SCHOLASTIC

ACTIVE™ Grammar

Practice Book 8

AF516238

Rosemary Allen

Name ______________________________

Class ______________________________

Previously published as Grammar Skills 8 by Learners Publishing Pte Ltd.

First edition 2012
Reprinted 2012, 2013, 2014 (twice), 2015, 2016, 2017, 2018, 2020, 2022, 2024, 2025

ISBN 978-81-8477-753-6

To Teachers and Parents

The study of English grammar in schools is changing as educators become increasingly aware of the important role context plays in language learning. The functional use of grammar has become a feature of English syllabuses around the world.

Active Grammar Practice Books have been written specifically to provide students with valuable links between basic, traditional grammatical concepts and the functional contexts in which they are used. The activities represent a blend of traditional and functional approaches to describe how texts 'work' in real-life situations and why certain grammatical choices are considered appropriate. Traditional grammar serves to provide students with the special terminology needed to talk about grammar, while functional grammar is intended to improve communicative competence by showing students how grammar works in the context of different text types.

The exercises in this book give students systematic guidance in developing an understanding of grammatical concepts. Panel notes are included to give hints for correct usage and highlight exceptions to grammar rules, as well as provide simple non-technical definitions to help students understand the exercises. The exercises incorporate learner-centred activities and are graded. Challenging ones are incorporated to motivate as well as interest the students.

It is hoped that teachers will find this series a valuable tool in their teaching programme, one that will provide students with a fascinating journey into the world of English language and a sound knowledge of how it works.

 ISBN 978-81-8477-753-6

Contents

 ISBN 978-81-8477-753-6

1 Concrete Nouns and Abstract Nouns

Grammar Help

- A **concrete noun** is the name of an object that you can see and touch. For example: *box, house, toys, flowers, rice, water.*
- Words for people and animals are also concrete nouns. For example: *child, teacher, players, cat, frog, mice.*
- An **abstract noun** is the name of something you cannot see or touch, such as a thought, a feeling, a quality or a period of time. For example: *idea, law, pain, happiness, age, health.*

A ***The box contains ten concrete nouns and ten abstract nouns. Write them in the correct columns below.***

apples	baker	coolness	danger	eagle
flour	gate	hours	hunger	kite
life	love	men	mountain	oil
patience	ruler	speed	trouble	work

Concrete		Abstract	
______	______	______	______
______	______	______	______
______	______	______	______
______	______	______	______
______	______	______	______

 ISBN 978-81-8477-753-6

Now use five of the concrete nouns and five of the abstract nouns in sentences of your own.

Concrete nouns

1. ______
2. ______
3. ______
4. ______
5. ______

Abstract nouns

1. ______
2. ______
3. ______
4. ______
5. ______

B ***Circle all the concrete nouns. Underline all the abstract nouns.***

1. Some people find it hard to make decisions.
2. The boys were riding their bicycles.
3. A lovely smell was coming from the kitchen.
4. We do not have enough time to finish this task.
5. They carried the piano with difficulty.
6. You should show more respect to your parents.
7. I had a very strange dream last night.
8. The woman took a key out of her pocket.
9. The departure of the train was delayed by twenty minutes.
10. She bought a can of cola at the shop.

 ISBN 978-81-8477-753-6

C ***Fill in each blank with an abstract noun from the box.***

courage	praise	sorrow	gratitude	confidence
anxiety	terror	regret	help	advice

1. You show _______________ by thanking someone.
2. You receive _______________ when you do something well.
3. You feel _______________ when you are very frightened.
4. You have _______________ when you are sure you can do something well.
5. You show _______________ by being brave.
6. You need _______________ when you are not sure what to do.
7. You feel _______________ when you are worried about something.
8. You express _______________ when you say you are sorry.
9. You give _______________ to people who are struggling to do something.
10. You show _______________ by crying.

Grammar Help

Concrete nouns can be countable or uncountable. (Remember that a countable noun can be singular or plural, and can be used with **a** or **an** in the singular. An uncountable noun does not have a plural form and cannot be used with **a** or **an**.)

- Here are some countable concrete nouns: *a* ***pencil****, an* ***orange****, some* ***people****, the* ***tigers****,* ***chairs****.*
- Here are some uncountable concrete nouns: *some* ***paint****, the* ***grass****,* ***cheese****.*

Abstract nouns can also be countable or uncountable.

- Here are some countable abstract nouns: *a* ***problem****, an* ***activity****, several* ***minutes****,* ***diseases****.*
- Here are some uncountable abstract nouns: *some* ***help****, the* ***music****,* ***excitement****.*

Some concrete and abstract nouns have both countable and uncountable uses in different contexts. For example: *They keep* ***chickens*** [countable] *in their yard. We had fried* ***chicken*** [uncountable] *for dinner. Computers have many different* ***uses*** [countable]. *The* ***use*** [uncountable] *of calculators in exams should be forbidden.*

 ISBN 978-81-8477-753-6

D ***Look at the nouns in bold print in this passage. Write CC in the brackets if the noun is concrete and countable. Write CU if the noun is concrete and uncountable. Write AC if the noun is abstract and countable. Write AU if the noun is abstract and uncountable.***

The government wants to build a new **airport** (   ) on some unused **land** (   ) close to our village. Last Friday the villagers had a **meeting** (   ) to discuss the matter.

Some **people** (   ) think that the airport will be a good thing for the community. It will bring **jobs** (   ) to an area that currently has a lot of **unemployment** (   ). It will also make foreign **travel** (   ) much easier.

Others are against the **idea** (   ). They say that the **noise** (   ) from the aircraft will disturb the villagers. They also think it will cause a lot more **traffic** (   ) on the roads.

E ***Here are ten concrete and abstract nouns that can be countable or uncountable. Write a pair of sentences containing each word, once as a countable noun and once as an uncountable noun. You can make the countable nouns plural if you like.***

1. (exercise) ____________________

   ____

2. (hair) ____________________

   ____

3. (size) ____________________

   ____

4. (paper) ____________________

   ____

5. (thought) ____________________

   ____

6. (surprise) ____________________

   ____

7. (metal) ____________________

   ____

 ISBN 978-81-8477-753-6

8. (accident) ______________________________

____

9. (stone) ______________________________

____

10. (fish) ______________________________

____

Grammar Help

- Some **abstract nouns** are formed by adding endings to adjectives or verbs. For example: *sad + ness =* ***sadness****; jealous + y =* ***jealousy****; equal + ity =* ***equality****; excite + ment =* ***excitement****; act + ion =* ***action****; appear + ance =* ***appearance****.*
- Sometimes you have to change or remove the last letters of the adjectives or verbs before you add the endings.
- You change **y** to **i** before adding **ness** if the adjective has two or more syllables. For example: *happ**y** → happ**iness*** but *shy → shyness.*
- You remove **t** from some adjectives before adding **ce**. For example: *patien**t** → patien**ce**; importan**t** → importan**ce**.*
- You remove **e** from adjectives and verbs before adding **ity, ion, ation, ance** or **al**. For example: *activ**e** → activ**ity**; educat**e** → educat**ion**; explor**e** → explor**ation**; guid**e** → guid**ance**; remov**e** → remov**al**.*
- You sometimes change **de** or **d** at the end of a verb to **s** before adding **ion**. For example: *exten**d** → exten**sion**; deci**de** → deci**sion**.*
- You change **ble** at the end of an adjective to **bility** at the end of the noun. For example: *reada**ble** → reada**bility**; possi**ble** → possi**bility**.*

F ***Complete the abstract nouns in these sentences with the endings from the box, using each one only once.***

ance	ation	dom	ence	ion
ment	ness	th	ty	y

1. The **warm**______________ of the animal's body melted the ice.
2. The police praised the **honest**______________ of the boys.

 ISBN 978-81-8477-753-6

3. Prisoners are deprived of their **free**_______________.
4. Jack made a very good **impress**_______________ on the judges.
5. The final **perform**_______________ of the show is on Saturday evening.
6. The accident was caused by the driver's **careless**_______________.
7. To our **amaze**_______________, the stain had completely disappeared.
8. Please state your **prefer**_______________: milk, cola or orange juice.
9. Officers rely on the **loyal**_______________ of their men.
10. They are meeting to discuss the **form**_______________ of a new team.

G ***Fill in each blank with an abstract noun formed from the given adjective or verb, using each of the endings in the box once or twice.***

ance	ce	ion	ity
y	ment	ness	

1. The children were punished for their _______________. (**naughty**)
2. A good _______________ is the best start you can have in life. (**educate**)
3. There is always a lot of _______________ in the city centre. (**active**)
4. The injured man needed emergency medical _______________ to save his life. (**treat**)
5. The red warning light indicates the _______________ of dangerous gases. (**present**)
6. The next _______________ of mail will be on Monday morning. (**deliver**)
7. That remark has no _______________ to the discussion. (**relevant**)
8. They came to the _______________ that he was lying. (**conclude**)
9. _______________ is a problem faced by some old people. (**lonely**)
10. You should take out travel _______________ when you go on holiday. (**insure**)

 ISBN 978-81-8477-753-6

H ***Fill in each blank with an abstract noun formed from one of the adjectives or verbs in the box.***

able	**amuse**	**consider**	**cruel**	**different**
disapprove	**exist**	**expand**	**foolish**	**persuade**

1. The __________ of ghosts has not yet been proved beyond doubt.
2. Some animals have the __________ to solve complex problems.
3. He never shows much __________ for other people's feelings.
4. What is the __________ between a star and a planet?
5. No amount of __________ will make me change my mind.
6. The charity was set up to protect children from __________ and neglect.
7. She could not hide her __________ at his funny voice.
8. Your __________ could have cost you your life.
9. Mrs Jones frowned in __________ at our behaviour.
10. Our science teacher explained why heat causes __________ of metals.

 ISBN 978-81-8477-753-6

2 Reflexive and Emphatic Pronouns

Grammar Help

- The **reflexive pronouns** are the eight pronouns that end in **self** or **selves**: *my**self**, your**self**, him**self**, her**self**, it**self**, our**selves**, your**selves*** and *them**selves***.
- You use a reflexive pronoun as the object of a verb when the object is the same person, animal or thing as the subject. For example: ***They** all enjoyed **themselves** at the funfair. **The cat** is washing **itself**.*
- You can also use a reflexive pronoun as the indirect object of a verb. For example: ***I** made **myself** a cup of tea. **Joe** should buy **himself** some new jeans.*
- The reflexive pronoun matches the subject in gender, person and number. For example, you use **herself** (feminine third person singular) as the object when **The girl** is the subject, and you use **ourselves** (first person plural) as the object when **We** is the subject.

A ***Fill in each blank with a reflexive pronoun from the box. You will need to use two of the words twice.***

myself	**yourself**	**himself**	**herself**
itself	**ourselves**	**yourselves**	**themselves**

1. Dad snored so loudly that he woke ____________________ up.
2. The machine switches ____________________ off automatically.
3. Help ____________________ to anything you want, children.
4. I told ____________________ not to be so silly.
5. My grandmother taught ____________________ to read and write when she was a little girl.
6. Sally and I congratulated ____________________ on solving the puzzle together.
7. Did you hurt ____________________, Mary?
8. John filled the basin with water and washed ____________________.
9. We could see ____________________ in the smooth surface of the still water.

 ISBN 978-81-8477-753-6

10. The boy's parents blamed ____________ for his accident.

Grammar Help

You also use a **reflexive pronoun** as the object of a preposition when it refers back to the subject of the sentence. For example: ***Sam** felt very pleased **with himself**. **The birds** made a nest **for themselves**.*

B ***Fill in each pair of blanks with a preposition from the box and a reflexive pronoun.***

about	**among**	**at**	**between**	**by**
for	**of**	**over**	**to**	**with**

1. Kate looked ____________ ____________ in the mirror.
2. I was cross ____________ ____________ for failing the exam.
3. Tom did not want to make a fool ____________ ____________.
4. The old lady seemed to be talking ____________ ____________.
5. Discuss the project ____________ ____________ before you begin.
6. The man was sitting ____________ ____________ on a park bench.
7. I lay on the bed and pulled the blanket ____________ ____________.
8. They sailed to the island and built a shelter ____________ ____________ there.
9. You should write a book ____________ ____________, Uncle Jack.
10. My brother and I divided the money ____________ ____________.

C ***Choose the correct pronoun to fill in the blanks.***

1. These two drinks are for Jane and ____________ (**you/yourself**).
2. I was trying to take a photo of ____________ (**me/myself**).
3. Sue cut ____________ (**her/herself**) on a piece of broken glass.
4. The women thanked ____________ (**us/ourselves**) for our help.

 ISBN 978-81-8477-753-6

5. 'You must try to express ____________ (**yourself/yourselves**) more clearly,' the teacher told the class.
6. Paul and ____________ (**I/myself**) will help you tidy the room.
7. The owl was grooming ____________ (**itself/himself**) with his beak.
8. The people who caused this damage should be ashamed of ____________ (**them/themselves**).
9. Carol pointed to the boy who had kicked ____________ (**her/herself**).
10. The company advertises ____________ (**itself/themselves**) on the Internet.

Grammar Help

You sometimes use the pronouns ending in **self** or **selves** for emphasis. They can be called **emphatic pronouns** when they are used in this way.

- An emphatic pronoun can follow the subject of a sentence. For example: *I **myself** prefer tea to coffee. The books **themselves** are not for sale, just the bookcase.*
- It can also come at the end of the sentence, still referring back to the subject. For example: ***I** prefer tea to coffee **myself**. Did **you** write that song **yourself**?*
- You sometimes use an emphatic pronoun to refer back to the object of a verb or preposition. *I have never met **the prime minister himself**. The book has been signed by **the author herself**.*
- An emphatic pronoun can be removed without changing the meaning of the sentence or making it sound incomplete. For example: *I ~~myself~~ prefer tea to coffee. Did you write that song ~~yourself~~? The book has been signed by the author ~~herself~~.*

D ***Is the word in bold print being used as an emphatic pronoun or as a reflexive pronoun? Write E (for emphatic) or R (for reflexive) in the brackets.***

1. You should feel proud of **yourself** for getting such a high mark. ( )
2. The animals scratch **themselves** on the rough bark of the trees. ( )
3. The president **himself** presented the prizes. ( )
4. Jane didn't want to go to the concert by **herself**. ( )
5. The light **itself** does not use much electricity. ( )

 ISBN 978-81-8477-753-6

6. I would have done it differently **myself**. ( )
7. We found **ourselves** a comfortable place to sit. ( )
8. The frame is more valuable than the picture **itself**. ( )
9. Peter hates watching **himself** on videos. ( )
10. The children made all the decorations **themselves**. ( )

E ***Rewrite each of these sentences, adding the given emphatic pronoun in the correct place.***

1. Carol and I had to do most of the work.

   (ourselves) ______________________________

2. The letter was not from the queen, but from one of her ladies-in-waiting.

   (herself) ______________________________

3. These buildings are older than the farmhouse.

   (itself) ______________________________

4. I do not believe in ghosts.

   (myself) ______________________________

5. Did you make these cakes?

   (yourselves) ______________________________

6. The festival takes place tomorrow.

   (itself) ______________________________

7. Give the letter to Dr Green.

   (himself) ______________________________

8. We did not see the statues, just pictures of them.

   (themselves) ______________________________

9. You must pay for the ticket.

   (yourself) ______________________________

10. The singer was good but the rest of the group were awful.

    (herself) ______________________________

 ISBN 978-81-8477-753-6

F ***Fill in each blank with the correct reflexive or emphatic pronoun.***

Mrs Smith has a busy life, looking after her home and family. She gets very little time to ________________. She and her husband have four children. Their youngest child, Paul, is just six months old so he cannot do anything for ________________. (He sometimes tries to feed ________________, but he makes a terrible mess!) Jane, who is almost three, has just learnt how to dress ________________. However, she still needs help with other things.

The other two children are twins, aged six. They are old enough to amuse ________________ when their mother is busy looking after their younger brother and sister. When their father comes home from work, he always asks them if they have behaved ________________ that day.

Mrs Smith does not go out to work ________________. 'I have too much to do at home,' she says. 'The house will not clean ________________, and meals will not cook ________________. I have to do all these things ________________.'

Mr Smith worries that his wife works too hard. 'You must take care of ________________, as well as us,' he says. Last weekend he stayed at home with the younger children while Mrs Smith took the twins on an outing. 'Enjoy ________________!' he said as they left.

 ISBN 978-81-8477-753-6

G ***Write sentences of your own containing the given verb and a reflexive or emphatic pronoun. Do not use the same pronoun more than once.***

1. (consider) ______________________________

____

2. (laugh) ______________________________

____

3. (hear) ______________________________

____

4. (move) ______________________________

____

5. (go) ______________________________

____

6. (protect) ______________________________

____

7. (take) ______________________________

____

8. (have) ______________________________

____

 ISBN 978-81-8477-753-6

3 Relative Pronouns

Grammar Help

- The words **that**, **which** and **who** can be used as **relative pronouns**. A relative pronoun introduces a piece of information about something or someone.
- You use **that** or **which** to say something more about a thing, animal or place you have just mentioned. For example: *I have read the book* ***which*** *you lent me. You will find the tools* ***that*** *you need in the shed.*
- You use **who** to say something more about a person you have just mentioned. For example: *Jane thanked the woman* ***who*** *helped her. The boy* ***who*** *won the race received a gold medal.*
- The part of a sentence introduced by a relative pronoun is called a **relative clause**. It can come at the end of the sentence or in the middle of the sentence. For example: *Tom pointed to the cake* ***that he wanted****. The cake* ***that Tom wanted*** *was the biggest on the plate.*

A ***Fill in the blanks with who or which.***

1. An ostrich is a bird ________________ cannot fly.
2. The man ________________ lives next door has a large dog.
3. Jane applied for a job ________________ was advertised in the newspaper.
4. The sandals ________________ I bought on holiday are very comfortable.
5. I shall give a prize to the boy or girl ________________ collects the most litter.
6. People ________________ are allergic to milk cannot eat cheese.
7. The picture ________________ Jack painted was much better than mine.
8. There were not enough tickets for everyone ________________ wanted to go to the concert.
9. The necklace ________________ the thief stole was not very valuable.
10. The waitress ________________ served us had curly hair.

 ISBN 978-81-8477-753-6

B ***Use the relative clauses in the box to complete the sentences below.***

that are not addressed to you	**that Jane saw**
that you have made	**which Dad gave her**
which I need	**which we throw away**
who broke the window	**who fixed the roof**
who have university degrees	**who need it most**

1. Graduates are people ______________________________.
2. You should not open letters ______________________________.
3. Some of the things ______________________________ could be recycled.
4. The boy ______________________________ offered to pay for the repair.
5. The book ______________________________ is on the top shelf.
6. They should give the money to the people ______________________________.
7. The bird ______________________________ had pointed wings.
8. Mum did not like the birthday present ______________________________.
9. The men ______________________________ said it will not leak anymore.
10. Please tidy up the mess ______________________________.

C ***Complete each sentence by adding a suitable relative clause.***

1. An architect is a person ______________________________.
2. An elephant is an animal ______________________________.
3. Ink is a liquid ______________________________.
4. A dictionary is a book ______________________________.
5. A liar is someone ______________________________.
6. An emperor is a man ______________________________.
7. A shark is a fish ______________________________.
8. A doctor is a person ______________________________.

 ISBN 978-81-8477-753-6

9. A waitress is a woman ______________________________.

10. Rice is a plant ______________________________.

Grammar Help

- The relative clauses we have looked at so far help to identify a particular person or thing. They are an essential part of the sentence that cannot be left out, and they are sometimes called **defining relative clauses**.
- Another type of relative clause, sometimes called a **non-defining relative clause**, adds extra information that is not essential. This type of relative clause has a comma before it, and another comma after it if it comes in the middle of the sentence. For example: *I sit next to Alice,* ***who is my best friend****. Polar bears,* ***which live in the Arctic,*** *have very thick fur.*
- You can use either **that** or **which** to introduce a defining relative clause about a thing, animal or place. For example: *This is the ring* ***that*** *Tom gave me. This is the ring* ***which*** *Tom gave me.*
- However, you cannot use **that** instead of **which** at the beginning of a non-defining relative clause. For example: *I live in North Street,* ***which*** *(NOT* ***that****) is near the station.*

D ***Five of these sentences contain non-defining relative clauses. Insert the missing commas.***

1. We visited Paris which is the capital of France.
2. Point to the book which you want.
3. My father who speaks very good English translated the notice.
4. I took the camera that I found to the police station.
5. Is that the boy who kicked you?
6. The person who wrote this book knows a lot about aircraft.
7. Sally washed her hands which were dirty and combed her hair.
8. Mr Brown who is our science teacher explained how computers work.
9. He sells most of the pictures that he paints.
10. The film stars Brad Pitt who is my favourite actor.

 ISBN 978-81-8477-753-6

E ***Rewrite each pair of sentences as a single sentence by making the second sentence a non-defining relative clause. The first one has been done as an example.***

1. Mr Black has a large dog. It guards his house.

   Mr Black has a large dog, which guards his house.

2. Sally helped the boy. He thanked her.

   ____

3. I have lost my favourite necklace. It was a present from my aunt.

   ____

4. Dad took his car to the garage. The car needed servicing.

   ____

5. We gave some food to the children. The children looked hungry.

   ____

6. Tom would not climb the ladder. He is afraid of heights.

   ____

7. They stayed at the Grand Hotel. It is in the town centre.

   ____

8. Our neighbour offered to look after our pets. He likes animals.

   ____

9. The Nile is the longest river in the world. It is in Africa.

   ____

10. I am going to visit my grandmother. She is in hospital.

    ____

 ISBN 978-81-8477-753-6

F ***Rewrite these sentences, adding a non-defining relative clause from the box to each one. The first one has been done as an example.***

which are nocturnal birds	**which is made of gold**
~~which was full of groceries~~	**which was not locked**
which was our grandfather's name	**who fixed it**
who have no children	**who is a doctor**
who is a strong swimmer	**who look exactly the same**

1. The van crashed into a tree.
   The van, which was full of groceries, crashed into a tree.
2. Dad left his car with the mechanic.
3. This ring belonged to my grandmother.
4. The girl opened the door.
5. The twins enjoy confusing people.
6. Mr and Mrs Brown let us play in their garden.
7. During the night we saw several owls.
8. Uncle Joe tried to rescue the boy.
9. My sister called her baby David.
10. I showed the rash to my uncle.

 ISBN 978-81-8477-753-6

G ***Use these relative clauses in sentences of your own. Write five sentences with defining relative clauses and five with non-defining relative clauses.***

that you sent me	that I bought yesterday
who has a broken ankle	who eat too much
which have eight legs	who lives in that house
who clapped and cheered	which was not very good
which is on the table	who do dangerous work

1. ____________________
2. ____________________
3. ____________________
4. ____________________
5. ____________________
6. ____________________
7. ____________________
8. ____________________
9. ____________________
10. ____________________

Grammar Help

- The words **which** and **who** can also be used as interrogative pronouns. For example: ***Who*** *is your favourite actor? I don't know* ***which*** *is the correct answer.* Do not confuse this use with the use of **which** and **who** as relative pronouns.
- The word **that** can also be used as a demonstrative pronoun or in indirect speech. For example: ***That*** *is the wrong answer. Joe told me* ***that*** *he felt ill.* Do not confuse these uses with the use of **that** as a relative pronoun.

 ISBN 978-81-8477-753-6

H ***Circle the relative pronouns in the following passage.***

A thief stole Grandma's handbag, which contained a lot of money, as she was walking home from the bank. She went to the police station and reported the theft to the officer who was standing behind the desk. The officer asked her to describe the man who had robbed her.

'He had long dark hair which looked as if it hadn't been washed for weeks,' said Grandma, 'and the jeans that he was wearing had holes in the knees.' She added that the man had a distinctive tattoo, which looked like a lizard, on his right arm.

'From that description,' said the officer, 'I think I know who the thief might be. It sounds like Joe Green, who has committed many similar crimes in the past.'

He showed Grandma a book that contained photos of various criminals and asked her which of the photos looked most like the thief. The pictures did not have names under them, but Grandma immediately pointed to the one of Joe Green. 'That is the man!' she said.

I ***Now write out the relative clauses on the lines below.***

____

____

____

____

____

 ISBN 978-81-8477-753-6

4 Linking Verbs

Grammar Help

A **linking verb** introduces a fact about someone or something. This person or thing is the subject of the verb. Unlike action verbs, linking verbs do not tell us what people or things do. Linking verbs tell us what they are or what they are like.

- The most frequent linking verb is **be**. As a linking verb, it can be followed by a noun, an adjective, an adverb or a prepositional phrase. For example: *I **am** afraid. David **is** the winner. We **were** upstairs. The car **was** in the garage.*
- Other linking verbs include **become, feel, go, turn, get, grow, look, appear, seem, sound, smell** and **taste**. Most of these can be followed only by adjectives when they are used as linking verbs. For example: *The cheese **went** mouldy. The wind **grew** stronger. That **sounds** interesting. Lemons **taste** sour.*
- However, a few linking verbs can also be followed by nouns. For example: *Joe **became** a doctor. Your hair **looks** a mess. I **felt** a complete idiot.*
- The adjective, noun, adverb or phrase that follows a linking verb is called its **complement**.

A ***Fill in each blank with a linking verb from the box in the past tense. Use each verb only once.***

smell	seem	become	look	be
sound	feel	grow	get	go

1. The winner ______________ the new record-holder for the 100-metre sprint.
2. The audience ______________ rather impatient.
3. Paul's plan ______________ sensible.
4. Sally ______________ the oldest student in her class.
5. It ______________ a shame to waste all the leftover food.
6. The light ______________ green and the car drove away.
7. I ______________ cold waiting at the bus stop.

 ISBN 978-81-8477-753-6

8. Jane ________________ a fool in her fancy-dress costume.
9. The rotting vegetables ________________ awful.
10. Dad ________________ very smart in his new suit.

B ***Complete each sentence with a suitable complement.***

1. Mrs Jones is ______________________ at our school.
2. The fruit tasted ______________________ so I did not eat it.
3. The students grew ______________________ as the day of the exam approached.
4. The liquid turned ______________________ when the powder was added.
5. The caterpillar became ______________________.
6. Mary seems ______________________ in her new job.
7. The sky went ______________________ and it began to rain.
8. The garden looks ______________________ at this time of year.
9. Tom appeared ______________________ when he read the letter.
10. My voice sounds ______________________ because I have a sore throat.

Grammar Help

- A number of **linking verbs** can also be used as action verbs. For example: *The flower* ***smelt*** *lovely* [linking verb]. *I* ***smelt*** *the flower* [action verb]. *Mary* ***looked*** *sad* [linking verb]. *Mary* ***looked*** *at me* [action verb].
- Do not confuse these two uses. Remember that a linking verb has a complement, which is usually an adjective. An action verb has an object, which is usually a noun, if it is transitive. Intransitive action verbs may be followed by adverbs or prepositional phrases.

C ***Look at the verbs in bold print in these sentences. If they are* linking *verbs, write* L *in the brackets. If they are* action *verbs, write* A.**

1. Sally **felt** (   ) ill so she **went** (   ) home.
2. Jane **turned** (   ) round as Mark **appeared** (   ) at the door.
3. When I **grow** (   ) up I want to **be** (   ) a doctor.

 ISBN 978-81-8477-753-6

4. Mr Smith **looked** (   ) in the mirror and noticed that his hair was **turning** (   ) grey.
5. The puzzle **looked** (   ) difficult but it **was** (   ) actually quite easy.
6. The weather **grew** (   ) colder as we **travelled** (   ) north.
7. The alarm will **sound** (   ) if an intruder **enters** (   ) the building.
8. It **smelt** (   ) smoky in the room for ages after the fire **went** (   ) out.
9. I **felt** (   ) the towel to find out if it **was** (   ) dry.
10. Dad **seemed** (   ) calm but Mum **sounded** (   ) worried.

D ***Write sentences of your own using the given verbs as linking verbs in any tense or form.***

1. (feel) ______________________________
2. (turn) ______________________________
3. (become) ______________________________
4. (get) ______________________________
5 (smell) ______________________________
6. (look) ______________________________
7. (seem) ______________________________
8. (be) ______________________________
9. (sound) ______________________________
10. (taste) ______________________________

E ***Now write sentences using five of these verbs as action verbs.***

1. ______________________________
2. ______________________________
3. ______________________________
4. ______________________________
5. ______________________________

 ISBN 978-81-8477-753-6

Grammar Help

- You cannot use the verb **be** as an action verb, but you can use it as a helping verb in continuous tenses and in the passive voice. For example: *I **am** wearing my new sandals. The dogs **were** barking. The gates **are** locked at six o'clock. The winner **was** given a silver trophy.*
- Do not confuse this use of **be** with its use as a linking verb. For example: *The house **was** very old* [linking verb]. *The house **was** destroyed by the fire* [helping verb]. *The joke **was** quite amusing* [linking verb]. *The comedian **was** amusing the audience with his jokes* [helping verb].

F ***Look at all the forms of the verb be in these sentences. Circle those that are linking verbs.***

1. Paul is in the bathroom.
2. The children were entertained by a clown.
3. Mary was taller than Kate when they were younger.
4. The study is used as a bedroom when guests are staying overnight.
5. Sally is a better tennis player than her brother is.
6. The boat was full of people who were going on holiday.
7. I could not finish the jigsaw because some of the pieces were missing.
8. This is the dress I am wearing for Sue's wedding.
9. Some of the workers are unpaid and others are paid very little.
10. The programme was interesting but it went on for too long.

 ISBN 978-81-8477-753-6

G Underline all the linking verbs in this passage.

It was Tom's birthday, and some of his friends were coming for lunch. He decided to make some soup with the vegetables that grew in his garden. He was not a very good cook, but he had found a recipe on the Internet that sounded easy enough.

The recipe told him to chop the vegetables and cook them in water until they went soft. Then he had to blend the mixture in the food processor. He did this, but unfortunately, he forgot to put the lid on the food processor before turning it on. The contents went all over the kitchen, and Tom began to feel rather stressed.

He cleared up the mess, then began again. This time he had more success. The soup did not look very appetizing, but it smelt delicious. Tom tasted the soup and decided that it needed a bit more salt. He tried to sprinkle just a little into the pan, but the top came off the container and far too much fell in. The soup became very salty indeed. In fact, it was inedible.

Tom grew even more frustrated and annoyed. He did not have enough time or ingredients to make any more soup. So he took a couple of pizzas out of the freezer and cooked those instead.

 ISBN 978-81-8477-753-6

5 Infinitives

Grammar Help

The **infinitive** of a verb has two forms: the **bare infinitive** and the **to-infinitive**.

- The **bare infinitive** is the base form used after the helping verb **do** and the modal verbs **can**, **could**, **will**, **shall**, **would**, **should**, **may**, **might** and **must**. For example: *I do not **like** strawberries. Does this book **belong** to you? The teacher will **be** angry with us. Can Tom **play** the piano?*
- You also use the bare infinitive after verbs such as **let**, **make**, **see**, **hear**, **feel**. For example: *Let's **go** to the park. Mum made me **clean** up the mess. Nobody saw Jack **leave** the room. I heard the door **open**.*

A ***Fill in the blanks with the bare infinitives from the box.***

be	break	enjoy	fit	pass
rain	run	stay	steal	touch

1. These shoes do not ________________ me.
2. The weatherman said it might ________________.
3. You must not ________________ in the school corridor.
4. I felt something ________________ my arm.
5. Did everyone ________________ the party?
6. Kate's parents let her ________________ up late on Saturdays.
7. The dish will ________________ if you drop it.
8. I saw the man ________________ the woman's purse.
9. People should ________________ kind to animals.
10. Could you ________________ me the salt, please?

 ISBN 978-81-8477-753-6

B ***Fill in each blank with any suitable bare infinitive.***

1. What did you ____________ Joe for his birthday?
2. I shall ____________ you outside the cinema.
3. Sally heard someone ____________ her name.
4. This shop does not ____________ children's books.
5. The flight will ____________ from Gate 26.
6. You should not ____________ litter on the ground.
7. They felt the floor ____________ beneath their feet.
8. My grandmother can ____________ six different languages.
9. The teacher made me ____________ my poem to the class.
10. She was afraid that the dog would ____________ her.

C ***Circle all the infinitives in this box.***

opened	eat	lying	comes	wrote	try
were	bring	find	has	go	learnt
walks	thought	swim	like	listens	miss
hoped	be	ride	forgot	teach	jumps
sew	driven	put	grown	win	close
mend	sold	drew	is	wear	rang

D ***Now write ten sentences of your own, using one of these verbs as a bare infinitive in each sentence. Try to use a variety of different verbs before the infinitives.***

1. ____________________
2. ____________________
3. ____________________
4. ____________________
5. ____________________

 ISBN 978-81-8477-753-6

6. ______________________________

7. ______________________________

8. ______________________________

9. ______________________________

10. ______________________________

E ***At the end of each sentence, write the bare infinitive of the verb in bold print.***

1. Dad **bought** me a new computer. ____________
2. The children **ran** down the hill. ____________
3. This **is** the oldest building in the village. ____________
4. The dog **had** long ears and a short tail. ____________
5. She **lay** on the sofa reading a magazine. ____________
6. The plane **flies** across the Pacific Ocean. ____________
7. We **went** to the zoo yesterday. ____________
8. They **left** without saying goodbye. ____________
9. He **saw** something shiny on the floor. ____________
10. Did you hear what I **said**? ____________

 ISBN 978-81-8477-753-6

Grammar Help

The **to-infinitive** is the base form with **to** in front of it. For example: ***to*** *sing;* ***to*** *have;* ***to*** *eat;* ***to*** *be.*

- You sometimes use the **to**-infinitive after **wh**-words. For example: *Sue didn't know how* ***to work*** *the machine. The man showed us where* ***to sit****. Tell me what* ***to do****.*
- You use the **to**-infinitive after some adjectives, nouns and pronouns. For example: *We were glad* ***to be*** *home. Is it likely* ***to rain****? The students are eager* ***to learn****. It is time* ***to go****. I have a new book* ***to read****. The bear was looking for something* ***to eat****. The builders still have lots* ***to do****.*
- The **to**-infinitive is also used after many verbs. For example: *Mum taught me* ***to swim****. The baby began* ***to cry****. I am trying* ***to help*** *you. Sally wants* ***to come*** *with us.*
- The modal verb **ought** is followed by the **to**-infinitive, not the bare infinitive. For example: *She ought* ***to take*** *more exercise.*
- You use the bare infinitive after **need** and **dare** when they are modal verbs. For example: *He need not* ***pay*** *the full fare. She does not know whether she dare* ***trust*** *the man.* However, you use the **to**-infinitive when they are lexical verbs. For example: *He does not need* ***to pay*** *the full fare. She does not know whether she dares* ***to trust*** *the man.*
- The verb **help** can be followed by the **to**-infinitive or the bare infinitive. For example: *Jane helped me* ***tidy*** *the room. Jane helped me* ***to tidy*** *the room.*
- You can make a **to**-infinitive negative by putting **not** before the word **to**. For example: *He told us* ***not*** *to go. I was anxious* ***not*** *to upset her.*

F ***Fill in each blank with the correct form of one of the infinitives from the box, adding to where necessary.***

drink	feel	hurt	know	phone
read	rest	stay	take	tell

1. You ought ______________ this book. It's really interesting.
2. Peter did not ______________ the answer to the question.
3. Grandpa is tired. He needs ______________ for a while.
4. Would you like something ______________ with your lunch?
5. She dare not ______________ her parents what she has done.
6. The movement of the boat on the rough sea made me ______________ sick.

 ISBN 978-81-8477-753-6

7. Remind me ______________ Grandma when we get home.
8. The nurse told Alice that the injection would ______________ a bit.
9. They would not let us ______________ photos inside the museum.
10. The weatherman advised people ______________ indoors.

G ***Fill in the blanks with any suitable to-infinitives.***

1. They looked for a shady place ______________.
2. Dad helped me ______________ the puzzle.
3. Sam was eager ______________ making the model.
4. I do not have anything nice ______________ for the wedding.
5. Nobody was allowed ______________ the building.
6. It is unkind of you ______________ your little sister.
7. There are lots of games ______________ on this computer.
8. It began ______________ so we went inside.
9. Rich people ought ______________ money to the poor.
10. Do we need ______________ all the questions on the paper?

H ***Circle all the bare infinitives in this passage and underline all the to-infinitives.***

If you are keen to become a doctor, you must work hard at school. You need to pass all your exams so that you may go to medical school. It is particularly important to do well in science subjects such as biology and chemistry.

A good doctor will also have a caring personality. He or she should want to help people get well. Being a doctor is not easy, but it can be a very rewarding career for the right person.

 ISBN 978-81-8477-753-6

I ***There is an error in each of these sentences. Rewrite them correctly on the lines below.***

1. I tried lift the box but it was too heavy.

   ____

2. Paul did not came to my party.

   ____

3. They decided to not buy the car.

   ____

4. Jane's teacher made her to rewrite her essay more neatly.

   ____

5. You ought not be rude to your parents.

   ____

6. I told her that she needs not bring a sleeping bag.

   ____

7. Did Aunt Mary forgot your birthday again?

   ____

8. Dad prefers not drive in wet weather.

   ____

9. The dog does want not to go out.

   ____

10. The doctor advised the patient eat more healthy food.

   ____

 ISBN 978-81-8477-753-6

6 The Past Perfect Tense

Grammar Help

The **past perfect** tense consists of **had** (the helping verb) followed by the past participle of the main verb. For example: *Sally said she* ***had lost*** *her key. The train* ***had left*** *ten minutes before we arrived. The people* ***had*** *never* ***seen*** *a helicopter before.*

- You use the past perfect tense in indirect speech when what was actually said (the direct speech) contains a verb in the simple past or present perfect tense. For example: *He said, 'I* ***fell*** *off my bike.'* becomes *He said he* ***had fallen*** *off his bike.* and *He said, 'I* ***have hurt*** *my knee.'* becomes *He said he* ***had hurt*** *his knee.*
- You also use the past perfect tense to talk about something that happened before an action or event in the simple past. For example: *The person who* ***had picked*** *up the most litter received a prize. The men felt tired because they* ***had worked*** *hard all day.*
- Like the present perfect tense, the past perfect tense can be used with adverbs such as **just**, **already** and **never**. These adverbs usually go before the past participle. For example: *Mum* ***had just cleaned*** *the floor when the dog ran in with muddy paws. Tom said he* ***had already seen*** *the film.*

A *Complete each sentence with the past participle of the given verb.*

1. Paul read us a poem that he had _______________ (**write**) himself.
2. We were late and the show had already _______________ (**begin**).
3. The birds had all _______________ (**fly**) back to their nests.
4. The choir had _______________ (**sing**) the song many times before.
5. Dad waited until the truck had _______________ (**overtake**) our car.
6. Mum told me she had _______________ (**throw**) my old jeans away.
7. They had _______________ (**run**) all the way so they were out of breath.
8. Jack said he had _______________ (**see**) a bear in the woods.
9. Sue felt sick because she had _______________ (**eat**) too much ice cream.
10. Mr Brown had not _______________ (**speak**) to his brother since their argument two years earlier.

 ISBN 978-81-8477-753-6

11. She had ______________ (**undo**) the wrong rope so the boat was still tied to the jetty.
12. The dog yelped because someone had ______________ (**tread**) on its tail.

B ***Fill in each pair of blanks in this passage with the past perfect tense of a verb from the box.***

visit	remember	finish	arrive	come
do	forget	put	bring	travel

Tom was flying to England with his parents. They __________ never ______________ by plane before. Tom's mother was very anxious. On the way to the airport she asked her husband if he __________ ______________ to bring their passports and tickets. He assured her that he __________ not ______________ anything.

The family were not sure what to do when they reached the airport. Fortunately, Tom's uncle __________ ______________ with them to help them. He was an experienced traveller who __________ ______________ many different countries on business. He showed them where to go to check in for their flight.

After they __________ ______________ this, they went to wait in the departure lounge. Tom __________ ______________ a book to read, so he was not bored. His father began doing the crossword puzzle on the back page of his newspaper. He ______________ almost ______________ it by the time their flight was called.

Tom's mother, still feeling anxious, started chatting to a woman sitting next to her. The woman said that the last time she flew to England, the airline

 ISBN 978-81-8477-753-6

_______ _______________ her baggage on the wrong plane. This gave Tom's mother something new to worry about! She said that she would not be able to relax until they _______ _______________ safely at their hotel in London.

C ***Fill in the blanks with the given verbs, using one in the past perfect tense and one in the simple past tense.***

1. By the time I _______________ my umbrella the rain _______________. (**find, stop**)
2. Mr Green _______________ at the school for twenty years before he _______________. (**teach, retire**)
3. The robbers _______________ the jewels they _______________. (**sell, steal**)
4. We _______________ that someone _______________ up the mess. (**notice, clear**)
5. The sun _______________ when the farmer _______________ up. (**rise, get**)
6. Nobody _______________ any food so there _______________ nothing to eat. (**bring, be**)
7. Tom _______________ his grandmother the flowers that he _______________ for her. (**give, buy**)
8. She _______________ to phone me but she _______________ to do so. (**promise, forget**)
9. The wind _______________ so I _______________ off my jacket. (**drop, take**)
10. Carol _______________ everyone that she _______________ the competition. (**tell, win**)
11. Grandma _______________ down for a rest after she _______________ the house. (**sit, clean**)
12. They _______________ the door in case the prisoner _______________ to escape. (**lock, try**)

 ISBN 978-81-8477-753-6

D ***Fill in each blank with just, already or never, using each word four times.***

1. Grandpa said he had ________________ had so many birthday cards.
2. She screamed because she had ________________ noticed the spider.
3. Tom said he had ________________ had enough to eat.
4. Dad had ________________ taken the bread out of the oven so it was still hot.
5. The taxi driver had ________________ heard of the place his passenger wanted to go to.
6. Carol ran home to tell her parents but they had ________________ heard the news.
7. The sun had ________________ gone in by the time we reached the beach.
8. I had ________________ fallen asleep when the noise woke me.
9. Anna had ________________ played badminton before.
10. They said they had ________________ sold all the tickets for the concert.
11. Colin told me not to touch the door that he had ________________ painted.
12. He had ________________ learnt to speak English, despite having lived in the USA for several years.

E ***Change these sentences from direct speech to indirect speech, using the past perfect tense at least once in the new sentence.***

1. Paul said, 'It rained all week.'

   ____

2. 'I have bought you a present,' Sue told her brother.

   ____

3. 'The baby has just woken up,' said Michael.

   ____

4. 'Nobody offered to help,' complained Alice.

   ____

5. Joe said, 'I have spent all the money I earned.'

   ____

 ISBN 978-81-8477-753-6

6. 'Have you finished your homework?' Mum asked me.

____

7. 'I did not understand the question,' protested the boy.

____

8. My sister said, 'I have just had a phone call from someone I don't know.'

____

9. 'I was too ill to go to the party,' explained Sue.

____

10. 'Where did you put the milk you bought, David?' asked Sally.

____

F ***Complete these sentences in any appropriate way, using a verb in the past perfect tense. The first one has been done as an example.***

1. He could not unlock the case because he had lost the key.
2. There was a red mark on Peter's arm where ______________.
3. I did not know what time it was because ______________.
4. Sally felt better after ______________.
5. We cleared the table when ______________.
6. Jane showed me the picture that ______________.
7. The teacher did not begin the lesson until ______________.
8. Joe was hungry because ______________.
9. The police told the reporters that ______________.
10. Mum and Dad watched TV when ______________.
11. My camera would not work because ______________.
12. They ate some of the fruit that ______________.
13. I brushed my teeth after ______________.
14. The little girl was crying because ______________.

 ISBN 978-81-8477-753-6

7 Types of Adjectives and Their Order

Grammar Help

Adjectives can be divided into six different types, based on what they tell you about the noun.

- **Adjectives of size** tell you how big or small something or someone is. For example: a **tall** girl; a **thin** slice; a **long** journey; **shallow** water.
- **Adjectives of quality** tell you what something or someone is like. For example: an **easy** question; a **young** man; a **bright** star; an **ugly** monster.
- There are various **adjectives of shape**. For example: a **square** mat; a **pointed** hat; a **bent** nail.
- There are many **adjectives of colour**. For example: a **red** T-shirt; **green** leaves; **black** hair.
- **Adjectives of origin** or **nationality** tell you where someone or something comes from. For example: a **Chinese** boy; an **English** city; an **Italian** car.
- **Adjectives of material** tell you what something is made of. They sometimes have the same form as a noun. For example: a **wooden** bench; a **glass** jar; a **cardboard** box.

A *Write the adjectives from the box under the correct headings below.*

American	blue	Chinese	clever	deep	brown
different	European	metal	Italian	grey	leather
low	tiny	oblong	old	Pakistani	paper
popular	red	round	rude	tall	square
plastic	straight	thick	triangular	white	woollen

Size	Quality	Shape	Colour	Origin	Material
______	______	______	______	______	______
______	______	______	______	______	______
______	______	______	______	______	______
______	______	______	______	______	______
______	______	______	______	______	______

 ISBN 978-81-8477-753-6

B ***Now use twelve of the adjectives from A (two of each type) to complete the following sentences.***

1. A ______________ shape has no corners.
2. France is a ______________ country.
3. The water is ______________ in the middle of the ocean.
4. ______________ people have lots of friends.
5. Tomatoes go ______________ when they ripen.
6. My ______________ jeans have holes in the knees.
7. There were ______________ bars at the windows of the prison cell.
8. The sun was shining and the sky was ______________.
9. Skyscrapers are ______________ buildings.
10. ______________ writing has symbols that stand for whole words.
11. The ______________ spoon melted in the heat of the flame.
12. You can use a ruler to draw a ______________ line.

C ***Fill in each blank in this passage with a suitable adjective of the type given in brackets. Do not use the same adjective more than once.***

Elephants are ______________ (**size**) animals that live in Africa and Asia. They have ______________ (**colour**) skin that feels ______________ (**quality**) because it is not covered with fur like the skin of some other mammals.

An elephant's ______________ (**size**) trunk is its nose, but it is not just used for breathing and smelling. The trunk is ______________ (**quality**) enough to lift ______________ (**quality**) objects, such as the logs that are used to make ______________ (**material**) buildings in some countries.

 ISBN 978-81-8477-753-6

At the sides of an elephant's mouth are two ________________ (**shape**) tusks that are ________________ (**shape**) at the ends. The tusks are actually teeth and they are made of a ________________ (**colour**) substance called ivory.

An elephant's ears are ________________ (**shape**) in shape. The ears of an ________________ (**nationality**) elephant are larger than those from Asia. This is one way in which you can tell the difference between the two animals.

D ***Expand each of these short sentences by adding an adjective before the noun. Then say what type of adjective you have added. You should add at least one adjective of size, quality, shape, colour, origin and material. The first one has been done as an example.***

1. The boy ate the bread. The **hungry** boy ate the bread. (**quality**)
2. This plant has berries. ________________ ( )
3. The insect crawled up the wall. ________________ ________________ ( )
4. Jane brushed her hair. ________________ ( )
5. The children were punished. ________________ ( )
6. He works in a car factory. ________________ ( )
7. I put the apples in a bag. ________________ ( )
8. She left a note for her mother. ________________ ________________ ( )
9. Tom was wearing his jacket. ________________ ( )
10. There was a mirror in every room. ________________ ________________ ( )
11. I found a coin on the ground. ________________ ( )
12. Jack does not like cheese. ________________ ( )

 ISBN 978-81-8477-753-6

Grammar Help

You sometimes put two or more adjectives before a noun. If the adjectives are of different types, you usually put them in the following order:

size – quality – shape – colour – origin – material

For example: *a **small plain white** handkerchief; a **strange pointed black** hat; a **beautiful Japanese silk** kimono.*

- If you use two or more adjectives of quality before a noun you put commas between them. For example: *a **kind, generous** woman; an **old, dirty, smelly** boot.*
- If you use two adjectives of colour before a noun, or two adjectives of any type after a linking verb, you put the word **and** between them. For example: *a **red and white** flag; The animal's eyes were **small and black**.*
- If you use three adjectives of colour before a noun, or three adjectives of any type after a linking verb, you put a comma between the first and second adjectives and the word **and** between the second and third. For example: *a **red, white and blue flag**; The animal's eyes were **small, bright and black**.*

E ***Complete these sentences by putting the given adjectives in the correct order. Add a comma or the word and where necessary. The last two questions have more than one correct answer.***

1. He was wearing a ________________ shirt. (**cotton thin**)
2. Lemons have ________________ skin. (**thick yellow**)
3. They were sent on an ________________ mission. (**dangerous exciting**)
4. London and Manchester are ________________ cities. (**busy English**)
5. A ________________ carpet covered the floor. (**orange purple**)
6. The library is a ________________ building. (**concrete huge modern**)
7. He stuck a ________________ label on the package. (**rectangular small white**)
8. Sue's hair is ________________. (**black long straight**)
9. Michael is a ________________ boy. (**honest intelligent polite**)
10. The travellers were ________________. (**cold tired wet**)

 ISBN 978-81-8477-753-6

F ***Write ten sentences of your own. Each sentence must contain a noun with two adjectives in front of it. These adjectives should be of different types, such as size and colour. Your set of sentences should contain at least one adjective of every different type: size, quality, shape, colour, origin and material. Do not use the same adjective more than once.***

For example:

An elephant is a **large grey animal** with a long trunk.

1. ______________________________
2. ______________________________
3. ______________________________
4. ______________________________
5. ______________________________
6. ______________________________
7. ______________________________
8. ______________________________
9. ______________________________
10. ______________________________

G ***Each of these sentences contains one or more errors relating to the groups of adjectives. Rewrite them correctly on the lines below.***

1. Mum was knitting a warm and woollen scarf.

   ____

2. My English young cousin is coming to stay.

   ____

3. The soup was hot, spicy, delicious.

   ____

4. She was wearing large gold round earrings.

   ____

5. Dad showed us a black white photo of Grandma as a child.

   ____

 ISBN 978-81-8477-753-6

8 Forming Adjectives from Verbs

Grammar Help

You can add various endings to verbs to change them into adjectives.

- The endings **ant**, **ent**, **ive** and **ative** form adjectives that mean 'doing the action of the verb'. For example: *the **triumphant** team* (the team that **triumphs**); *a **different** word* (a word that **differs** from another); *a **disruptive** student* (a student who **disrupts** the class); *a **talkative** child* (a child who **talks** a lot).
- The endings **able** and **ible** form adjectives meaning 'that can receive the action of the verb'. For example: *a **washable** blanket* (a blanket that you can **wash**); ***flexible** plastic* (plastic that you can **flex**, or bend).
- The ending **ing** forms adjectives that have the meaning of the present participle. For example: *a **flattering** remark; **distressing** news.*
- The ending **ed** forms adjectives that have the meaning of the past participle. For example: *a **deserted** beach; a **wounded** man.* Irregular past participles can also be used as adjectives. For example: *her **swollen** ankle; a **spoilt** child.*

A ***Choose the correct ending to complete the adjectives in these sentences.***

1. The flash________________ (**ant, ing**) light means that the battery needs recharging.
2. Protect________________ (**ed, ive**) covers stop things from being damaged.
3. Absorb________________ (**ent, ible**) substances soak up liquid.
4. Sue put the neatly fold________________ (**able, ed**) clothes in her suitcase.
5. A repent________________ (**ant, ive**) person is sorry for what they have done.
6. Your stomach is part of your digest________________ (**ent, ive**) system.
7. Something that is buoy________________ (**able, ant**) floats in water.
8. The word 'house' is a count________________ (**able, ing**) noun.
9. Some people are frighten________________ (**ed, ible**) of spiders.
10. I tried not to disturb the sleep________________ (**ent, ing**) baby.
11. Persist________________ (**ent, ive**) people do not give up easily.
12. A convert________________ (**ed, ible**) car has a roof that folds away.

 ISBN 978-81-8477-753-6

Grammar Help

You sometimes have to make a spelling change when you add these endings.

- If the verb ends in **y** with a consonant in front of it, you change this to **i** before adding **ant**, **able** or **ed**. For example: *rely* → *rel**iant**, envy* → *env**iable**, hurry* → *hurr**ied**.*
- If the verb ends in **e** with a consonant in front of it, you usually remove the **e** before adding any of the adjective endings. For example: *ignore* → *ignor**ant**, revere* → *rever**ent**, abuse* → *abus**ive**, cure* → *cur**ative**, note* → *not**able**, collapse* → *collaps**ible**, pierce* → *pierc**ing**, engage* → *engag**ed**.* However, you sometimes add **able** to the whole verb, especially if it ends in **ce** or **ge**. For example: *notice* → *notice**able**, change* → *change**able**, like* → *like**able** or lik**able**.*
- If the verb ends in **consonant** + **vowel** + **consonant** (except **w**), and the vowel is stressed, you double the final consonant before adding **ent**, **able**, **ing** or **ed**. For example: *repel* → *repel**lent**, hug* → *hug**gable**, fit* → *fit**ting**, tan* → *tan**ned*** but *frighten* → *frighten**ing*** (the **e** is unstressed).
- If the verb ends in **d**, **de** or **re**, you change this to **s** before adding **ive** or **ible**. For example: *defen**d*** → *defen**sive**, divi**de*** → *divi**sible**, cohe**re*** → *cohe**sive**.*
- If a verb with three or more syllables ends in **ate**, you remove this before adding **ant** or **able**. For example: *domin**ate*** → *domin**ant**, irrit**ate*** → *irrit**able*** but *inflate* → *infl**atable*** (the verb has only two syllables).

B ***Write the adjective formed from the given verb and ending.***

1. adhere + ive = ______________
2. admire + able = ______________
3. affirm + ative = ______________
4. agree + able = ______________
5. appal + ing = ______________
6. comprehend + ible = ______________
7. control + able = ______________
8. convalesce + ent = ______________
9. cry + ing = ______________
10. debate + able = ______________
11. digest + ible = ______________
12. excel + ent = ______________
13. explode + ive = ______________
14. force + ible = ______________
15. imagine + ative = ______________
16. knot + ed = ______________
17. manage + able = ______________
18. observe + ant = ______________
19. stagger + ing = ______________
20. tolerate + ant = ______________

 ISBN 978-81-8477-753-6

21. decorate + ive = ________________

22. defy + ant = ________________

23. vary + able = ________________

24. worry + ed = ________________

C ***Complete these sentences with adjectives formed from the given verbs. All the endings you will need are in the box, but they are not in the correct order.***

able	able	ant	ed	ed	ent
ent	ible	ing	ing	ive	ive

1. ________________ parents give their children everything they ask for. (**indulge**)
2. A ________________ car does not break down. (**rely**)
3. ________________ news is not what you expected. (**surprise**)
4. A ________________ jacket can be worn inside out. (**reverse**)
5. ________________ athletes receive medals at the Olympic Games. (**win**)
6. A ________________ problem is one that happens over and over again. (**recur**)
7. ________________ people have no difficulty making up their minds. (**decide**)
8. A ________________ couple is a husband and wife. (**marry**)
9. ________________ people are good at designing and making things. (**create**)
10. You use wool to make ________________ garments. (**knit**)
11. A ________________ person does not act immediately. (**hesitate**)
12. A ________________ action is something you wish you had not done. (**regret**)

D ***Fill in each blank in this passage with a suitable adjective formed from the given verb.***

Jane felt ________________ (**bore**). Her brother Tom was at the leisure centre with his friends and she had nothing to do. She went upstairs and found her mother clearing out the attic.

 ISBN 978-81-8477-753-6

'Would you like me to help you?' asked Jane.

Her mother was ______________ (**delight**). 'Yes, please,' she replied. 'It's not a very ______________ (**please**) task, but it has needed doing for a long time. However, it's rather dusty up here, so it might be ______________ (**sense**) to put on your old jeans.'

Jane did as she was advised, then climbed the ladder into the attic. 'There is an ______________ (**impress**) collection of old books up here,' she said, picking up a large encyclopedia. 'Are any of them ______________ (**value**)?'

'I don't think so,' replied her mother. 'That book you are holding is very ______________ (**inform**), but it is rather out-of-date, and all the facts it contains can be easily found on the Internet these days.'

Jane opened a box and took out a ______________ (**frame**) photograph of a little boy with his parents. 'That is a picture of your grandfather when he was three years old,' said her mother. 'He is ______________ (**adore**)!' exclaimed Jane. 'My great-grandmother looks very ______________ (**attract**) too,' she added. 'I wish I had inherited her good looks!'

Just then Jane's mobile phone rang. It was an ______________ (**urge**) text message from her brother. 'Tom has missed his bus and wants you to collect him from the leisure centre,' she told her mother. 'While you're out I'll carry on sorting through this box. There's some ______________ (**fascinate**) stuff in here!'

 ISBN 978-81-8477-753-6

E ***Complete these sentences with adjectives formed from the verbs in the box. You should use each verb twice: once as a present participle and once as a past participle.***

amaze	annoy	depress	disgust	excite	fall	freeze	interest

1. The man bravely dived into the ______________ water.
2. The dolphins have learnt to perform some ______________ tricks.
3. I helped Dad to sweep up the ______________ leaves.
4. The film was very ______________ and the end was a real surprise.
5. Joe felt ______________ because he was sure he had failed the exam.
6. Sally has the ______________ habit of finishing other people's sentences.
7. You can buy ______________ vegetables at the supermarket.
8. There is nothing ______________ on TV at the moment.
9. Hundreds of ______________ viewers phoned the radio company to complain.
10. They ran home through the ______________ rain.
11. The ______________ children could not wait to open their presents.
12. Winter in England can be rather ______________ when the weather is cold and wet.
13. There were ______________ gasps from the audience as the magician's assistant disappeared.
14. I am not ______________ in science fiction.
15. The food looked and smelt ______________, so nobody wanted to eat it.
16. Mum will be ______________ if we are home late.

F ***Write sentences of your own using any adjective formed from the given verb. Do not use the same ending more than three times.***

1. (advise) ______________________________

____

2. (compare) ______________________________

____

 ISBN 978-81-8477-753-6

3. (complicate) ____________________

____

4. (depend) ____________________

____

5. (divide) ____________________

____

6. (expect) ____________________

____

7. (follow) ____________________

____

8. (glitter) ____________________

____

9. (offend) ____________________

____

10. (persuade) ____________________

____

11. (upset) ____________________

____

12. (weave) ____________________

____

 ISBN 978-81-8477-753-6

9 Comparison of Adverbs

Grammar Help

- There are three **degrees of comparison** of adverbs: **positive** (*high, gracefully*), **comparative** (*higher, more gracefully*) and **superlative** (*highest, most gracefully*).
- Some short adverbs of manner have the same form as the related adjectives. You use **er** and **est** to form the comparative and superlative of these adverbs. For example: *fast* – *fast**er*** – *fast**est***. You sometimes have to change the ending of the adverb. For example: *earl**y*** – *earl**ier*** – *earl**iest***; *close* – *clos**er*** – *clos**est***.
- You use **more** and **most** to form the comparative and superlative of longer adverbs, including all those formed by adding **ly** to an adjective. For example: *clearly* – ***more*** *clearly* – ***most*** *clearly*; *easily* – ***more*** *easily* – ***most*** *easily*.
- Some adverbs have **irregular** comparative and superlative forms. For example: *well* – *better* – *best*; *badly* – *worse* – *worst*; *far* – *further* – *furthest*.

A ***Underline all the comparative adverbs and circle all the superlative adverbs in these sentences. Do not underline or circle any comparative or superlative adjectives by mistake.***

1. Dad has been driving more carefully since his accident.
2. Speak louder so that those sitting furthest from the stage can hear you.
3. The wind blew more strongly during the night.
4. They had a competition to find out who could stay silent the longest.
5. You will feel warmer if you walk more quickly.
6. Paul was the most smartly dressed boy in the room.
7. Jane moved closer to the front of the classroom in order to see the board better.
8. Some stars shine more brightly than others.
9. Those who wrote the most neatly got the highest marks in the handwriting test.
10. The engine runs more smoothly when the car is newly serviced.

 ISBN 978-81-8477-753-6

B ***Write the positive, comparative and superlative forms of the adverbs related to these adjectives. The first one has been done as an example. Take care! Some of the adverbs have the same form as the adjective.***

	Adjective	Positive Adverb	Comparative Adverb	Superlative Adverb
1.	happy	happily	more happily	most happily
2.	bad			
3.	long			
4.	gentle			
5.	far			
6.	helpful			
7.	fast			
8.	noisy			
9.	hard			
10.	enthusiastic			
11.	comfortable			
12.	good			

Grammar Help

- You use the positive degree of adverbs with **as**. For example: *I whispered* ***as quietly as*** *I could.*
- You use the comparative degree with **than**. For example: *Some of the people were waiting* ***more patiently than*** *others.*
- You use the superlative degree with **the**. For example: *Which animal can jump* ***the highest****?*
- You can also put a comparative or superlative adverb before a past participle used as an adjective. For example: *This is a* ***more loosely*** *woven fabric. There will be a prize for the* ***most attractively*** *arranged vase of flowers.*

 ISBN 978-81-8477-753-6

C ***Complete each sentence with the positive, comparative or superlative form of the given adverb.***

1. The pilot flew the helicopter as ____________________ as he dared. (**low**)
2. The southern part of the country is ____________________ populated than the north. (**densely**)
3. Sally is the youngest child but she shouts the ____________________! (**loud**)
4. The concert was ____________________ attended this year than it was last year. (**well**)
5. Jack fought as ____________________ as a soldier. (**bravely**)
6. The team played ____________________ than they have ever played before. (**badly**)
7. I do not see my grandparents as ____________________ as I would like to. (**often**)
8. The person who gave the ____________________ was not a rich man. (**generously**)
9. They should treat their workers ____________________ than they do. (**kindly**)
10. Spread the butter as ____________________ as you can. (**thinly**)
11. Which of the students travels the ____________________ to school? (**far**)
12. We had a race to see who could run the ____________________. (**fast**)

D ***Read the short passage in the box. Then fill in the blanks in the following sentences with the correct positive, comparative or superlative forms of the adverbs early, late, quickly and slowly. Do not use the same form of the same adverb more than once.***

> Paul, Jane, Mary and Sam set off from school at four o'clock to walk to the park. Because they walked at different speeds, they all reached the park at different times. Paul arrived at 4:15, Jane arrived at 4:20, Mary arrived at 4:25 and Sam arrived at 4:30.

1. Sam walked the ____________________.
2. Mary did not arrive as ____________________ as Sam did.

 ISBN 978-81-8477-753-6

3. Nobody else walked as ________________________ as Sam did.
4. Mary did not arrive the ________________________.
5. Paul walked ________________________ than everyone else.
6. Jane arrived ________________________ than Sam.
7. Mary did not walk as ________________________ as Paul.
8. Sam arrived ________________________ than both the girls.
9. Jane did not arrive as ________________________ as Paul did.
10. Mary walked ________________________ than Jane.
11. Paul arrived the ________________________.
12. Jane did not walk the ________________________.

E ***Fill in each blank in this passage with the positive, comparative or superlative form of an adverb in the box.***

high	**close**	**heavily**	**early**	**soon**
soundly	**far**	**badly**	**hard**	**well**

It began to rain at midday, ________________________ than the forecasters had predicted. The villagers who lived by the river were worried about flooding, as the water was already near the top of the banks. All afternoon they worked as ________________________ as they could preparing their flood defences. Those who lived the ________________________ to the river were in the greatest danger, so they were helped by those who lived ________________________ away.

By nightfall it was raining even ________________________, and the villagers knew they would not sleep as ________________________ as usual that night. Some of the residents of Marsh Lane (which had been the

 ISBN 978-81-8477-753-6

____________ affected during the last flood) did not go to bed at all. They knew that their houses were ____________ protected this time, but they still took the precaution of moving as many possessions as possible upstairs.

During the night the river rose ____________ and eventually overflowed its banks. However, by the time the villagers woke the rain had stopped. Most of the roads were under water but little serious damage had been done. Everything returned to normal much ____________ than it had after the great flood of the previous year.

F ***Write sentences of your own using the given adverbs in the positive, comparative or superlative degree.***

1. (eagerly) ____________
2. (honestly) ____________
3. (cheaply) ____________
4. (hard) ____________
5. (easily) ____________
6. (well) ____________
7. (close) ____________
8. (politely) ____________
9. (angrily) ____________
10. (sweetly) ____________
11. (long) ____________
12. (nicely) ____________

 ISBN 978-81-8477-753-6

10 Adverbial Phrases

Grammar Help

An **adverbial phrase** is a group of two or more words used together to tell you more about the action of a verb. The phrase itself does not contain a verb.

- An adverbial phrase of **manner** tells you how the action is performed. It often consists of two adverbs: an adverb of degree followed by an adverb of manner. For example: *A cheetah can run* ***very quickly****. I solved the puzzle* ***quite easily****.* It may also consist of a comparative or superlative adverb of manner. For example: *A cheetah can run* ***more quickly*** *than a gazelle can. Who solved the puzzle* ***the most easily****?* It is sometimes a longer phrase. For example: *Kate writes* ***with her left hand****. They spoke* ***as quietly as possible****.*
- An adverbial phrase of **place** tells you where the action is performed. It sometimes consists of two adverbs of place. For example: *I walked* ***back home****. Is it any cooler* ***out there****?* However, it most often consists of a preposition followed by a noun phrase. For example: *He swam* ***across the river****. Does this bus go* ***to the station****?*
- An adverbial phrase of **time** tells you when the action is performed. For example: *I saw an interesting TV programme* ***yesterday evening****. The bank closes* ***at half past five****.*
- An adverbial phrase of **frequency** tells you how often the action is performed. For example: *I visit my grandparents* ***twice a month****. You should wash your hair* ***more often****.*
- An adverbial phrase of **duration** tells you how long the action is performed for. For example: *Mr Brown has taught at this school* ***since 1990****. We waited* ***for half an hour*** *and then we left.*

A ***Underline all the adverbial phrases in these sentences.***

1. I went to bed and fell asleep straight away.
2. The man hit the nail with a hammer and drove it into the wood.
3. This time last week we were sitting on the beach.
4. You have only just missed the bus. It left two minutes ago.
5. Last August I flew to England to visit my relatives.
6. They worked hard all morning and finally finished at midday.

 ISBN 978-81-8477-753-6

7. In cold countries people dress more warmly when they go out.
8. My best friend has moved to another town, so I see her less often than I used to.
9. Yesterday afternoon our teacher took us to the museum.
10. We arrived too early so we had to wait outside the cinema.

B ***Fill in each blank with one of the adverbial phrases from the box.***

very reluctantly	**three times a day**	**for several weeks**
after lunch	**during the performance**	**at a restaurant**
hardly ever	**on Saturday mornings**	**little by little**
fifty years ago	**into small pieces**	**by the phone**

1. It ____________________ snows in this part of the world.
2. The doctor told me to take the medicine ____________________.
3. I am going to the shopping mall ____________________.
4. ____________________ I take my little sister to the playground.
5. We usually have dinner ____________________ on Mum's birthday.
6. He sat ____________________, waiting for it to ring.
7. Jack has been reading that book ____________________.
8. Chop the vegetables ____________________.
9. ____________________ the plant grew into a tall strong tree.
10. ____________________ there was much less traffic on the roads.
11. The shopkeeper ____________________ gave the customer her money back.
12. You are not allowed to take photos ____________________.

C ***Look at the adverbial phrases in bold print in this passage. Write M in the brackets after adverbial phrases of manner. Write P after adverbial phrases of place. Write T after adverbial phrases of time. Write F after adverbial phrases of frequency. Write D after adverbial phrases of duration.***

Tom has been learning the violin **since his tenth birthday** (   ), when he received the instrument as a birthday present. **Once a week** (   ) he has a

 ISBN 978-81-8477-753-6

violin lesson **at home** ( ). His teacher, Miss Lee, comes **to his house** ( ) **on Friday evenings** ( ). She has been playing the violin **for many years** ( ) and has performed **at the city's concert hall** ( ) **several times** ( ). Needless to say, she plays **much more skilfully** ( ) than Tom does **at the moment** ( ). However, he practises **very hard** ( ) **every day** ( ) before he goes **to school** ( ). He gets up **at 6:30** ( ) and plays his violin **from 7:00 to 8:00 a.m.** ( ) **in his bedroom** ( ). His sister **quite often** ( ) knocks **on the wall between their rooms** ( ) and asks him to play **more quietly** ( ) so that she can sleep **a little longer** ( ).

D ***Use one word from each box to make up two-word adverbial phrases to complete these sentences.***

A:	at	extremely	for	in	last	more
	over	quite	straight	to	tomorrow	since

B:	bed	casually	evening	fast	home	hours
	midnight	politely	September	there	work	year

1. Please put the boxes ______________ ______________.
2. Supersonic aircraft travel ______________ ______________.
3. Mum came ______________ ______________ after my phone call.
4. Where did you go for your holidays ______________ ______________?
5. Our neighbour usually drives ______________ ______________.
6. The clock strikes twelve times ______________ ______________.
7. I asked them ______________ ______________ to make less noise.
8. There is a concert at the theatre ______________ ______________.
9. The dog has been barking ______________ ______________.

 ISBN 978-81-8477-753-6

10. People often dress ____________ ____________ at the weekends than they do during the week.
11. I have not seen my aunt and uncle ____________ ____________.
12. Sally likes reading ____________ ____________.

E ***Write sentences of your own containing the given adverbial phrases about things that you do (or things that you have done). You do not have to tell the truth!***

1. (at school) ________________________________
2. (without difficulty) ________________________________
3. (during the evening) ________________________________
4. (twice a year) ________________________________
5. (very rarely) ________________________________
6. (at half past seven) ________________________________
7. (last week) ________________________________
8. (in my bedroom) ________________________________
9. (very well) ________________________________
10. (for eight hours) ________________________________

Grammar Help

- Like adverbs, adverbial phrases can occupy three different positions in a sentence. For example: *The dog ran* ***across the road*** (end position). *The doctor* ***very gently*** *examined the patient* (mid position). ***At the end of this term*** *we have an important maths exam* (initial position).
- Some transitional devices that come at the beginning of a sentence are also adverbial phrases. For example: ***Strictly speaking,*** *a spider is not an insect.* ***All in all,*** *the mission was a great success.*

 ISBN 978-81-8477-753-6

F ***Rewrite these sentences, adding a suitable adverbial phrase to each one. Try to use at least one example of each type of adverbial phrase (manner, place, time, frequency, duration) and at least one example of each position (end, mid, initial).***

1. I washed the porcelain vase.

   ____

2. The boys were playing football.

   ____

3. They carried the injured player on a stretcher.

   ____

4. She asked him to repeat the question.

   ____

5. I am having a party.

   ____

6. Jane ran to greet her grandparents.

   ____

7. Dad has a shower before breakfast.

   ____

8. It rained all day.

   ____

9. We learnt about polar bears today.

   ____

10. The phone rang several times.

    ____

 ISBN 978-81-8477-753-6

11 Complex Prepositions

Grammar Help

- A **complex preposition** (also called a **compound preposition**) is a short phrase that is used as a preposition. It links the noun or pronoun which follows it to what has gone before. Most complex prepositions are two or three words long. For example: *There were twenty passengers **on board** the plane. Jane stood **in front of** the mirror.*
- Some complex prepositions consist of an adverb, a conjunction or another type of word followed by a simple preposition. (A simple preposition is a single word such as **with** or **to**.) For example: *The dog ran **away from** its master* (adverb + preposition). *There will be no trains tomorrow **because of** the railway workers' strike* (conjunction + preposition).
- Some complex prepositions consist of a noun or another type of word between two simple prepositions. For example: *The captain accepted the trophy **on behalf of** the team. The bride and groom gave a small gift to each guest **in accordance with** tradition.*
- Complex prepositions are sometimes used at the beginning of a sentence, especially in formal writing. For example: ***Further to** your letter of complaint, the potholes in the road will be repaired later this month. **Contrary to** the weather forecast, the sun shone all day.*

A *Underline the complex prepositions.*

1. We lost the match because of Jane's poor performance in goal.
2. You had better keep away from me in case you catch my cold.
3. There has been an improvement in exam results compared with those of previous years.
4. My little brother has just learnt to count up to a hundred.
5. People pay different amounts of tax depending on their income.
6. The caretaker has all the keys other than the one for this room.
7. According to the timetable the train should arrive at 7:50.
8. Alternative sources of energy such as solar power do less harm to the environment.
9. There was no furniture in the room apart from the chair I was sitting on.

 ISBN 978-81-8477-753-6

10. The boy jumped on to the train as it moved away.
11. He made several mistakes owing to his lack of experience.
12. The food we have bought, together with what we already have, will be more than enough.

B ***Use the words in the box to complete the complex prepositions in these sentences.***

addition	far	aid	relation	accordance	case
reference	front	well	top	means	comparison

1. A noun sometimes has an adjective in ______________ of it.
2. I'll go with you as ______________ as the crossroads.
3. They communicated with each other by ______________ of sign language.
4. The bird's head is small in ______________ to its body.
5. With ______________ to your advertisement, I would like to buy the camera you have for sale.
6. Sally had to miss a turn in ______________ with the rules of the game.
7. We have a comfortable life in ______________ with many less fortunate people.
8. The suitcase is on ______________ of the wardrobe.
9. The workers receive a bonus in ______________ to their annual salary.
10. I took the mobile phone with me in ______________ of emergency.
11. The house has a study and a playroom upstairs as ______________ as four large bedrooms.
12. Jack is going on a sponsored walk in ______________ of charity.

 ISBN 978-81-8477-753-6

C ***Draw lines to match each complex preposition with a simple preposition that has the same meaning.***

COMPLEX PREPOSITIONS	SIMPLE PREPOSITIONS
on board	beside
close to	about
in favour of	despite
other than	aboard
in spite of	without
by means of	for
next to	on
on top of	near
prior to	from
but for	by
with regard to	before
out of	except

D ***Now use six of these complex prepositions in sentences of your own.***

____

____

____

____

____

____

 ISBN 978-81-8477-753-6

E ***Choose the correct word to complete the complex prepositions.***

1. I made the cake **according** ______________ (**to/with**) the recipe.
2. We finished the work **ahead** ______________ (**on/of**) schedule.
3. The thief was arrested **along** ______________ (**with/for**) his two accomplices.
4. Nobody **apart** ______________ (**from/for**) Mary offered to help.
5. **Contrary** ______________ (**with/to**) popular opinion, the disease is not infectious.
6. We shall have lunch in the dining room or on the patio, **depending** ______________ (**with/on**) the weather.
7. Everyone had left **except** ______________ (**for/from**) Jane and Tom.
8. You will find the atlas **in** ______________ (**beside/between**) the dictionary and the encyclopedia.
9. Our apartment block is quite small **in comparison** ______________ (**from/with**) the skyscrapers in the city centre.
10. They walked along the path **as far** ______________ (**from/as**) the bridge over the canal.
11. Everyone must pay the same fare **regardless** ______________ (**of/to**) their age.
12. The shop will stay open until eight o'clock **as** ______________ (**at/from**) Monday 15 October.

F ***Fill in each blank in this letter with a complex preposition from the box.***

close to	**with regard to**	**such as**	**instead of**	**on behalf of**
as well as	**in view of**	**next to**	**in favour of**	**in spite of**

Dear Sir

I am writing ______________ the people of this town ______________ the new supermarket which is to be built ______________ the industrial estate.

 ISBN 978-81-8477-753-6

We do not think this store is needed in the town. We already have two large supermarkets ______________ many smaller shops.

The council approved this plan ______________ considerable opposition from the residents. Only a small minority are ______________ the new supermarket. Most would prefer to see a leisure centre built on the site. This would give the young people of the town somewhere to go ______________ hanging around the streets.

The new store could cause other problems, ______________ traffic congestion as shoppers enter and leave its large car park. People living ______________ the site will also have to put up with a lot of noise and inconvenience during the construction work. ______________ these objections I hope you will reconsider this proposal.

Yours faithfully

Robert Green

G ***Complete each sentence with any suitable complex preposition. Do not use the same phrase more than once.***

1. He carried on running ______________ the pain in his chest.
2. The flight was delayed ______________ bad weather.
3. I have no warm clothing ______________ this jumper.
4. A baby bird has fallen ______________ the nest.
5. You should not eat unhealthy snacks ______________ your meals.
6. Jane tied the baggage label ______________ her suitcase.
7. Dad carries an extinguisher in his car ______________ fire.
8. Paul put sugar in the soup ______________ salt, by mistake.

 ISBN 978-81-8477-753-6

9. She has her elderly parents to look after __________ four young children.

10. Carol went __________ the boy and asked him if he needed any help.

11. I was standing __________ the prince but he did not speak to me.

12. Aunt Mary lives __________ a famous writer.

 ISBN 978-81-8477-753-6

12 Prepositional Phrases

Grammar Help

A **prepositional phrase** is a preposition followed by a noun, a pronoun or a noun phrase. For example: *They went* ***to bed****. This letter is* ***for you****. Mark sits* ***next to Paul****.*

- You sometimes use prepositional phrases as adverbs, to say more about the action of the verb, such as where or when it happened. For example: *We ate our sandwiches* ***at the station****. The dog ran* ***out of the house****. She did not get home* ***until seven o'clock****. It rained heavily* ***during the afternoon****.*
- You can also use prepositional phrases as adjectives, to say more about a noun or to make it clear which person or thing you are talking about. For example: *Dad bought Mum a box* ***of chocolates****. All the DVDs* ***on this shelf*** *are mine. Have you seen a man* ***with a large black dog****?*
- You sometimes use prepositional phrases as the complement of the linking verb **be**, to say more about the subject of the verb. For example: *Mary is* ***at school****. The horses were* ***in their stable****.*
- You can use prepositional phrases after some adjectives. For example: *There is something wrong* ***with the television****. My sister is fond* ***of animals****.*
- Some sentences contain two or more prepositional phrases used one after another. For example: *Colin went* ***to the park*** */* ***after lunch****. I took a pencil* ***from the top drawer*** */* ***of my desk****. We waited* ***for you*** */* ***outside the cinema*** */* ***until five o'clock****. There were two people* ***ahead of me*** */* ***in the queue*** */* ***at the post office****.*

A ***Underline all the prepositional phrases in this passage. Then circle the prepositions that introduce them.***

The president arrived at the electronics factory in a large black car. The owners of the company, Mr and Mrs Kim, were waiting by the door to greet him. Their important visitor arrived on time, at exactly ten o'clock.

Mr and Mrs Kim invited the president into their office for coffee before his tour of the factory. Then they showed him around the main building, where

 ISBN 978-81-8477-753-6

their most complex products are made. He chatted to the workers and seemed very interested in the manufacturing process.

As he left, the president said that he was extremely impressed by Mr and Mrs Kim's company. He said it was the most efficiently run factory he had visited during his three years as president.

B ***Draw lines to match the main part of each sentence with the correct prepositional phrase to complete it.***

1. The spider crawled •	• due to sickness.
2. My brother is •	• since last April.
3. Jane apologized •	• on the piano.
4. Please give this letter •	• than Kate.
5. The boat sailed •	• up the wall.
6. Peter would like an apple •	• at work.
7. Mr Smith played the tune •	• to your parents.
8. Several people were absent •	• by the river.
9. We went for a walk •	• of cake.
10. I have not seen Michael •	• under the bridge.
11. The boy was eating a large slice •	• for her mistake.
12. Alice is taller •	• instead of a banana.

 ISBN 978-81-8477-753-6

C ***Fill in each pair of blanks with a preposition from box A and a noun, pronoun or noun phrase from box B. Use each word or phrase only once.***

A	**about**	**above**	**at**	**away from**	**because of**	**by**	**for**	**from**
	in	**next to**	**off**	**on**	**out of**	**to**	**with**	**without**

B	**a grey suit**	**a tree**	**flour**	**football**	**her purse**	**herself**
	mine	**my uncle**	**Sally**	**Saturday**	**them**	**the bank**
	the city centre	**the fireplace**		**the noise and traffic**		**the road**

1. Grandma took some money ________ ________________.
2. The animals seemed to know that we had food ________ ________________.
3. A postcard ________ ________________ arrived this morning.
4. Tom likes reading stories ________ ________________.
5. ________ ________________ we visited Buckingham Palace.
6. The car skidded ________ ________________ and collided ________ ________________.
7. My sister's bedroom is ________ ________________.
8. You can't make bread ________ ________________.
9. The woman was talking ________ ________________.
10. We moved ________________ ________________ ________________ ________________.
11. The man ________ ________________ works ________ ________________.
12. The picture ________ ________________ was painted ________ ________________.

D ***Look at the prepositional phrases in bold print in these sentences. If the phrase is being used as an adverb, write Adv in the brackets. If it is being used as an adjective, write Adj.***

1. The baby did not cry **during the night**. ( )
2. Mrs Jones gave everyone a bag **of sweets**. ( )
3. The pain **in my back** is getting worse. ( )
4. Paul ran **to the bus stop** as fast as he could. ( )
5. She poured some milk **into her coffee** and stirred it. ( )
6. The children washed their hands **in the stream**. ( )
7. I saw a girl **with long hair** running away. ( )
8. Is this the road **to the station**? ( )
9. Put the stool **under the table**. ( )
10. The postman handed me a parcel **from my grandmother**. ( )
11. Joe unlocked the door **with his key**. ( )
12. I watched a programme **about dinosaurs** yesterday evening. ( )

E ***Complete each sentence with a suitable prepositional phrase. Try to use as many different prepositions as you can.***

1. The supermarket does not close ____________________.
2. Jack fell ____________________ and hurt his ankle.
3. The rocks rolled ____________________.
4. 'It doesn't matter,' she said ____________________.
5. I sent a text message ____________________ when I heard the good news.
6. The woman wore a gold chain ____________________.
7. He heard a strange noise ____________________ and went to investigate.
8. I found the missing book ____________________.
9. She laid a blanket ____________________.
10. The car stopped ____________________.
11. I am reading an interesting book ____________________.

 ISBN 978-81-8477-753-6

12. Kate is studying medicine ______________________.

F ***Write sentences of your own containing the given prepositional phrases.***

1. (with a sharp knife) ______________________

2. (to the zoo) ______________________

3. (in your wardrobe) ______________________

4. (about our holidays) ______________________

5. (of the box) ______________________

6. (to America) ______________________

7. (since this morning) ______________________

8. (behind the sofa) ______________________

9. (during the English lesson) ______________________

10. (by train) ______________________

11. (in front of me) ______________________

12. (for lunch) ______________________

 ISBN 978-81-8477-753-6

G ***Complete these sentences by adding two of the prepositional phrases from the box to each one.***

about road safety	**above ours**	**at the end**	**at the gate**
by the policeman	**from her trip**	**in the apartment**	**in the garden**
of the letter	**on his new bike**	**on the lake**	**to the birds**
to the man	**until sunset**	**up the lane**	**with a bad cold**

1. Mr and Mrs Green live ______________________________.
2. Joe cycled ______________________________.
3. I signed my name ______________________________.
4. The children were throwing food ______________________________.
5. My parents like to sit ______________________________.
6. Show your ticket ______________________________.
7. Carol came back ______________________________.
8. We were given advice ______________________________.

 ISBN 978-81-8477-753-6

13 Phrasal Verbs

Grammar Help

A **phrasal verb** is a verb followed by one or two other words that give it a particular meaning. These other words are adverbs or prepositions, and they are called the **particles** of the phrasal verb. For example: the phrasal verb **close down** (verb + adverb) means 'stop doing business'; the phrasal verb **bump into** (verb + preposition) means 'meet by chance'; the phrasal verb **do away with** (verb + adverb + preposition) means 'get rid of'.

- If the particle of the phrasal verb is a preposition, it always comes straight after the verb. For example: *Dad* ***bumped into*** *an old schoolfriend at the theatre. Do these football boots* ***belong to*** *you?*
- If the particle is an adverb and the verb is intransitive, the particle always comes straight after the verb. For example: *A crowd gathered to watch the spacecraft* ***blast off****. The shop* ***closed down*** *because it did not have enough customers.*
- If the particle is an adverb and the verb is transitive, you usually put the particle after the object. For example: *Ali* ***blew*** *the candles* ***out****. Sue* ***put*** *the box* ***down****.*
- However, you sometimes put an adverb particle before the object of a transitive verb, especially when the object is a long noun phrase, or when it has a relative clause attached to it. For example: *Ali* ***blew out*** *all the candles on his birthday cake. Sue* ***put down*** *the box that she was carrying.*
- You cannot put an adverb particle before a personal pronoun. You can say, '***Switch off*** the radio,' '***Switch*** the radio ***off***' or '***Switch*** it ***off***,' but you CANNOT say, '***Switch off*** it.'

A ***Fill in each blank with one of the phrasal verbs from the box.***

agree with	**bring back**	**call on**	**care for**
carry out	**die down**	**do away with**	**fall for**
give away	**grow out of**	**run through**	**pull together**

1. Let's ____________________ the last verse of the song again.
2. I ____________________ everything you have said.

 ISBN 978-81-8477-753-6

3. My younger cousin gets my clothes after I ________________ them.
4. Our new friends promised to ________________ us if they ever came to our town.
5. Looking at old photos can ________________ happy memories.
6. If we all ________________ the work will soon be done.
7. The old man had nobody to ________________ him.
8. Please don't ________________ my secret!
9. The government is planning to ________________ identity cards.
10. No sensible person would ________________ such a silly trick.
11. We waited for the storm to ________________ before leaving.
12. Don't make threats that you cannot ________________.

B ***Draw lines to match each phrasal verb with the correct definition.***

PHRASAL VERB		DEFINITION
1. put out	•	• forget to take
2. take after	•	• stop working
3. draw up	•	• close completely
4. stand for	•	• enter
5. keep up with	•	• extinguish
6. change into	•	• continue
7. break down	•	• represent
8. go in for	•	• become
9. block off	•	• go as fast as
10. carry on	•	• distinguish between
11. leave behind	•	• write
12. tell apart	•	• be like

 ISBN 978-81-8477-753-6

C ***Now use each of the phrasal verbs in B in a sentence of your own.***

1. ______
2. ______
3. ______
4. ______
5. ______
6. ______
7. ______
8. ______
9. ______
10. ______
11. ______
12. ______

D ***Look at the phrasal verbs in bold print. Write A in the brackets if the particle is being used as an adverb. Write P if the particle is being used as a preposition.***

1. Kate **stood by** her brother when everyone else was against him. ( )
2. You should **read** your essay **through** carefully to check for spelling mistakes. ( )
3. She **took off** her jacket and hung it on a peg. ( )
4. They are **banking on** our help. ( )
5. We need to find a better way of **putting across** our argument. ( )
6. I lay on the grass and watched the clouds **pass by** in the sky above. ( )
7. Paul **went off** peanuts after eating a bad one that made him sick. ( )
8. Aunt Mary **takes in** stray cats. ( )
9. I hope I **get through** all my exams this year. ( )
10. Jane **came across** an opened letter when she was tidying her desk. ( )
11. Dad **switched on** the radio to listen to the news. ( )
12. I don't **believe in** ghosts. ( )

 ISBN 978-81-8477-753-6

E ***All these sentences contain phrasal verbs beginning with come. Fill in each blank with one of the particles from the box.***

apart	between	down	into	from
of	off	out	round	up

1. Mum washed the tablecloth but the stain did not come ______________.
2. Good friends should not let minor arguments come ______________ them.
3. There was a thorough investigation, but nothing came ______________ it.
4. She did not buy the necklace, hoping that the price would come ______________ in the sale.
5. The handle came ______________ when I turned it.
6. I was going to ask Paul about his trip but the subject did not come ______________.
7. Jack came ______________ some money when his grandfather died.
8. Some patients feel sick when they come ______________ after an operation.
9. If you don't use the right glue, the model will come ______________.
10. This song comes ______________ the musical 'Cats'.

F ***Use the verbs in the box in the correct tense or form to complete the phrasal verbs in this passage.***

attend	come	fall	get	go	lie
look	pass	pick	set	stand	wake

Mrs Lee was a very busy woman. She had four children to ______________ after, as well as her husband and her elderly father who lived next door.

One day, Mrs Lee ______________ up feeling unwell, but she knew that she could not stay in bed. She ______________ up at the usual time and made breakfast for her family. After the older children had ______________ off

 ISBN 978-81-8477-753-6

for school, and her husband had gone to work, she _______________ down for a short rest. Then her baby son started crying, so she had to go and _______________ to him. She had just put him back in his cot when the phone rang. It was her father. He had _______________ down in his kitchen and needed her help.

Mrs Lee _______________ up the baby and went next door. Her father's ankle was badly swollen, so she took him to the hospital. The emergency department was busy that day and they had to wait for two hours before a doctor was free. This meant that Mrs Lee, who had not had any breakfast that day, had to _______________ without lunch as well.

When she finally _______________ up to leave, she _______________ out and fell to the floor. She _______________ to a few minutes later and saw her father's anxious face looking down at her. He said that he had phoned her husband at work, who was going to take a taxi to the hospital and drive them all home. Mrs Lee sighed with relief.

G ***Each sentence contains two phrasal verbs with missing particles. Choose two of the words in brackets to fill in the blanks.***

1. Passengers have to check _____________ two hours before the flight takes _____________. (**away**, **in**, **off**, **out**)
2. Sue looked _____________ the word in a dictionary to find _____________ what it meant. (**after**, **at**, **out**, **up**)
3. The teacher told Simon _____________ for answering her _____________. (**back**, **down**, **off**, **on**)
4. They are hoping that the culprit will come _____________ and own _____________. (**forward**, **in**, **out**, **up**)
5. I'll tell Dad to call you _____________ when he gets _____________ from work. (**away**, **back**, **in**, **to**)

 ISBN 978-81-8477-753-6

6. Mary picked __________ the coin and looked __________ it. (**at**, **into**, **off**, **up**)
7. We went __________ for a walk because we did not want to sit __________ all day. (**around**, **back**, **down**, **out**)
8. One of the boys fell __________ as he was running __________. (**away**, **for**, **over**, **to**)
9. Come __________ and sit __________. (**between**, **down**, **in**, **off**)
10. I could not work __________ the answer to the puzzle so I gave __________ trying. (**for**, **off**, **out**, **up**)

H ***All these sentences contain phrasal verbs ending with up. Fill in the blanks with the missing verbs.***

1. James __________ up a story about a bank robbery.
2. It's very noisy in here so you will have to __________ up.
3. The bus __________ up at the bus stop.
4. I need a pump to __________ up the tyres on my bike.
5. Kate used a calculator to __________ up the figures.
6. Everyone __________ up in fancy costumes for the carnival.
7. The orphaned children were __________ up by their grandparents.
8. Paul slowed down to let me __________ up.
9. __________ up your hand if you know the answer.
10. Grandpa __________ up painting as a hobby after he retired.

 ISBN 978-81-8477-753-6

14 Conjunctions

Grammar Help

Conjunctions are words or short phrases that link two parts of a sentence together. For example: *I have a cat* ***and*** *a dog. Jane dropped the cup* ***but*** *it did not break. Dad went to bed* ***because*** *he was tired. The cat will scratch you* ***if*** *you annoy it.*

A ***Underline the conjunctions in these sentences.***

1. I washed my hands before I ate my lunch.
2. The peaches were sweet and juicy.
3. We stayed indoors until it stopped raining.
4. Young babies cannot talk or dress themselves.
5. Do not ring the bell unless you need help.
6. Tom felt thirsty so he had a drink.
7. I have not stopped working since I got up this morning.
8. Alice has one brother but no sisters.
9. Joe screamed because he was frightened.
10. She read a magazine while she was waiting.

Grammar Help

The conjunctions **and, but, or** and **so** are called **co-ordinating conjunctions**. They link two words or sets of words that serve the same purpose in the sentence.

- You can use **and, but** and **or** to link two words that belong to the same class, such as two nouns, two adjectives or two verbs. For example: *Our teacher is* ***strict but fair****. I did not* ***hear or see*** *anything unusual.*
- You can also use **and, but** and **or** to link two phrases (or a word and a phrase) of the same class. For example: *I bought* ***a bag of flour and a bottle of milk****. She asked me* ***politely but very firmly*** *to make less noise.*

 ISBN 978-81-8477-753-6

- You can use **and**, **but**, **or** and **so** to link two clauses. (A clause is a set of words that contains a verb.) For example: *I may phone Sally* ***or*** *I may send her an email. He is deaf* ***so*** *he cannot hear you.*
- The conjunction **and** shows addition. For example: *Mary washed the dishes* ***and*** *Tom dried them.*
- The conjunction **but** expresses contrast. For example: *Mary washed the dishes* ***but*** *she did not dry them.*
- The conjunction **or** introduces an alternative: *Would you prefer to wash the dishes* ***or*** *dry them?*
- The conjunction **so** introduces an effect or result: *The dishes were wet* ***so*** *Tom dried them.*

B ***Fill in each blank with and, but, or or so. Use each word three times.***

1. Paul wants to be an engineer ______________ an architect when he grows up.
2. I need a new computer ______________ I cannot afford to buy one.
3. Carol had toothache ______________ she went to see the dentist.
4. He wrote his name quickly ______________ neatly.
5. Dad bought Mum a gold necklace ______________ a matching bracelet.
6. My hands were dirty ______________ I washed them.
7. The cruel man did not treat his animals kindly ______________ gently.
8. The horse jumped over the gate ______________ galloped away.
9. The mattress on this bed is firm ______________ comfortable.
10. I could not decide whether to read a book ______________ watch TV.
11. Anna's hair is long ______________ straight.
12. We did not have tickets ______________ we could not watch the match.

Grammar Help

Conjunctions such as **when**, **as**, **if** and **while** are called **subordinating conjunctions**. They link clauses, not words or phrases.

- The conjunctions **although**, **even though** and **even if** express contrast. For example: *I bought the book* ***even though*** *it was very expensive.*

 ISBN 978-81-8477-753-6

- The conjunctions **when, while, as, as soon as, before, after, since** and **until** are used to talk about time and sequence. For example: *Dad went to work by bus* ***while*** *his car was being repaired. The air got cooler* ***after*** *the sun went down.*
- The conjunctions **because, as, since** and **in case** introduce a reason. For example: *I couldn't have a cookie* ***as*** *there were none left.*
- The conjunctions **so that** and **in order that** introduce a purpose. For example: *We talked quietly* ***so that*** *we would not wake the baby.*
- The conjunctions **if** and **unless** introduce a condition. For example: *They should be here by six o'clock* ***unless*** *they miss the train.*
- The conjunctions **as** and **than** are used in comparisons. For example: *Jane cannot draw as well* ***as*** *Joe can. Oranges taste sweeter* ***than*** *lemons do.*

C ***Use the conjunctions in the box to complete these sentences. Do not use the same word or phrase more than once.***

as	because	before	even if	even though	if
in case	since	so that	than	unless	until

1. Mum will be angry ________________ you break this vase.
2. I shall not forgive him ________________ he says he is sorry.
3. The dog looked fierce ________________ it was wagging its tail.
4. Do not open the door ________________ the train stops.
5. This exercise is easier ________________ the last one was.
6. They took off their dirty shoes ________________ they went in.
7. Mary tore her jeans ________________ she climbed over the fence.
8. Take a map ________________ you get lost.
9. We shall go for a walk whatever the weather ________________ it rains.
10. He covered the bushes with nets ________________ the birds could not eat the fruit.
11. Grandma has lived in this house ________________ she was a little girl.
12. Everyone laughed at Joe ________________ he looked so funny.

 ISBN 978-81-8477-753-6

D ***Fill in each blank in this passage with a suitable co-ordinating or subordinating conjunction. Do not use the same word more than once.***

Dolphins live in the sea __________ they are not fish. They do not have gills __________ scales as fish do. Dolphins belong to a group of animals called mammals. Human beings __________ four-legged animals such as horses also belong to this group.

Most mammals cannot live in water. They would drown __________ they did not have air to breathe all the time. Dolphins do not breathe __________ they are underwater. They can stay below the surface __________ they do not have to breathe as often as we do.

Mammals differ from other groups of animals in various ways. They give birth to live young instead of laying eggs. The baby stays inside its mother's body __________ it is ready to be born. Its mother feeds it with milk __________ it is young.

Most mammals have hair all over their bodies, __________ human beings do not have enough to keep themselves warm. That is one of the reasons why people have to wear lots of clothes __________ they live in a hot country.

Grammar Help

Some words, such as **before**, **after**, **since**, **until**, **as** and **than**, can be used as conjunctions or prepositions. They are conjunctions when they are followed by a clause. They are prepositions when they are followed by a phrase. For example: *I waited* **until** *it went dark* (conjunction). *I waited* **until** *seven o'clock* (preposition). However, **and**, **but** and **or** are always conjunctions, even when they come before a word or phrase rather than a clause.

 ISBN 978-81-8477-753-6

E ***Look at the word or phrase in bold print in each sentence. If it is a co-ordinating conjunction, write CC in the brackets. If it is a subordinating conjunction, write SC. If it is a preposition, write P.***

1. She called for help **but** nobody heard her. ( )
2. Kate is two years older **than** Jack. ( )
3. We could not see very well **because** it was foggy. ( )
4. Mum went shopping **after** breakfast. ( )
5. I went to the zoo with my friend Carol **and** her mother. ( )
6. Joe missed the bus **so** he had to walk home. ( )
7. Michael has not seen his parents **since** he went to university. ( )
8. Grandpa has felt much better **since** his operation. ( )
9. I think these houses were built in 1984 **or** 1985. ( )
10. I'll make the tea **as soon as** the kettle boils. ( )
11. He spoke loudly **so that** everyone could hear. ( )
12. Several people left **before** the end of the show. ( )

F ***Complete these sentences in any appropriate way.***

1. I lost my key so ______________________________.
2. Jane did not know what to do because ______________________________.
3. Do not cross the road until ______________________________.
4. We could buy a bigger car if ______________________________.
5. Shall I help you or ______________________________?
6. He was wearing sunglasses although ______________________________.
7. The light comes on when ______________________________.
8. My sister has had a baby but ______________________________.
9. Tom repeated the question in case ______________________________.
10. Jane ran home as fast as ______________________________.
11. Colin switched off the TV and ______________________________.
12. You cannot go on the school trip unless ______________________________.

 ISBN 978-81-8477-753-6

15 Transitional Devices

Grammar Help

Transitional devices (connectors) are words or phrases that link sentences or parts of sentences together.

- Conjunctions are transitional devices. They are usually found in the middle of a sentence, but some subordinating conjunctions can go at the beginning instead. For example: *The baby woke up* ***when*** *the dog barked.* ***When*** *the dog barked, the baby woke up.*
- You can also put a co-ordinating conjunction at the beginning of a sentence for emphasis or dramatic effect. *I thought I heard someone talking in the next room.* ***But*** *I was alone in the house.*
- Some types of adverbs are transitional devices. They often link sentences together. For example: *There are two reasons why she left the job.* ***Firstly,*** *the pay was not very good.* ***Secondly,*** *one of her workmates was bullying her.*
- Some adverbial phrases can serve the same purpose. For example: *Jack is very rarely late.* ***On the contrary,*** *he is usually the first person to arrive.*
- Adverbs and adverbial phrases used to link sentences sometimes come in other parts of the second sentence. For example: *Mum and Dad said they were going out. They did not,* ***however,*** *tell us where they were going. There are various ways of saving money. You could buy fewer magazines,* ***for example.***

A ***Underline all the transitional devices in these sentences or pairs of sentences.***

1. My parents lived in a tiny apartment before I was born.
2. Ali does not speak English. He can, however, speak several other languages.
3. If the phone rings while I am out, please take a message.
4. Carol invited Paul to her party but he could not go.
5. You must leave the building as soon as you hear the fire alarm.
6. All the doors were locked. Therefore, the burglar must have got in through a window.
7. Dad put on his glasses in order to read the small print on the document.
8. It rained every day and the food in the hotel was not very good. It was a disappointing holiday, all in all.

 ISBN 978-81-8477-753-6

9. Most of these children are orphans. That is, they have no mothers or fathers.
10. You may have a cookie provided that you do not drop any crumbs on the carpet.
11. There were no melons on the fruit stall so Mum bought a pineapple instead.
12. First I mixed some fertilizer into the soil, then I sowed the seeds.

Grammar Help

Some transitional devices are pairs of words with other words between them.

- You use **either … or** to introduce two alternatives. For example: *You can **either** come with us **or** stay at home.* **Neither … nor** is the negative form of **either … or**. For example: ***Neither** Peter **nor** Jane saw what happened.*
- You use **so … that** and **such … that** to talk about a consequence or result. You put **so** before an adjective or adverb and **such** before a noun or noun phrase. For example: *I was **so** tired **that** I could not stay awake. Dad has **such** large feet **that** he has difficulty finding shoes to fit him.*

B ***Fill in the pairs of blanks in these sentences with either … or, neither … nor, so … that or such … that.***

1. You can wear the chain ____________ round your wrist ____________ round your ankle.
2. We were having ____________ a good time ____________ we didn't want to go home.
3. Jane had ____________ had a wash ____________ changed her clothes when her guests arrived.
4. The box was ____________ heavy ____________ I could not lift it on my own.
5. Paul has ____________ phoned me ____________ emailed me for weeks.
6. This jacket belongs ____________ to Sue ____________ to Kate, but I don't know which.
7. I have been reading ____________ a frightening story ____________ I shall probably have nightmares tonight.
8. She spoke ____________ quietly ____________ few people heard her.

 ISBN 978-81-8477-753-6

9. Colin was hoping to get ______________ a bike ______________ a computer for his birthday.
10. This camera is ______________ easy to use ______________ anyone can take good pictures with it.
11. The room was ______________ a mess ______________ it took ages to tidy it up.
12. A baker's shop sells ______________ fruit ______________ vegetables.

Grammar Help

Here is a reminder of the different uses of transitional devices.

- addition: *and, in addition (to), as well (as), together with, along with, also, too, moreover, furthermore, besides*
- alternative: *or, either … or, neither … nor, alternatively, instead*
- comparison: *as, than*
- contrast: *but, though, although, even though, even if, however, nevertheless, whereas, on the other hand, on the contrary*
- illustration: *for example, such as, namely, that is, in other words*
- consequence or result: *consequently, as a result, thus, so … that, such … that, otherwise*
- time and sequence: *first(ly), second(ly), third(ly), then, next, finally, before, after, while, when, as, as soon as, since, until, meanwhile, eventually*
- conclusion: *therefore, altogether, all in all, overall, in conclusion, to sum up, in short*
- reason: *because, as, since, in case*
- purpose: *so that, in order that, so, in order to*
- condition: *if, unless, provided that*

C ***Choose twelve transitional devices, including at least one from each of the groups in the box above, and write a sentence (or pair of sentences) of your own containing this word or phrase.***

1. ____
2. ____
3. ____
4. ____
5. ____

 ISBN 978-81-8477-753-6

6. ______________________________

7. ______________________________

8. ______________________________

9. ______________________________

10. ______________________________

11. ______________________________

12. ______________________________

D ***Fill in each blank in this passage with a word or phrase from the box.***

after	**and**	**as**	**as soon as**	**before**	**first**
however	**in order that**	**instead**	**meanwhile**	**or**	**otherwise**
so	**such as**	**that**	**then**	**when**	**while**

Mum and Dad are decorating my brother Jack's bedroom ______________ he is away on a school trip. ______________ he left, they asked him to choose some new wallpaper. His old wallpaper has cartoon characters on it, ______________ he is far too grown-up for such childish things now. ______________ his friends come to see him, he is ______________ embarrassed about the wallpaper ______________ he never takes them to his bedroom.

Jack said that he would like to have his bedroom walls painted ______________, in a plain colour ______________ dark blue ______________ black. My parents agreed to do this. They suggested, ______________, that a paler colour would make the room look lighter.

 ISBN 978-81-8477-753-6

_______________ Jack had gone, Dad set to work on the walls. _______________ he stripped off the old wallpaper, _______________ he made the surface smooth enough to paint on. _______________, Mum rubbed down the door and window frame with sandpaper _______________ she can repaint them.

That is all they have done so far. I hope they will manage to finish everything in time. _______________, Jack will have to share my bedroom _______________ he comes home. He will not be pleased about that, _______________ he says that I snore all night.

E ***Rewrite these pairs of sentences, adding a suitable transitional device in any appropriate position. Do not use the same word or phrase more than once. You can make the two sentences into one if necessary. You may need to change the wording of some of the sentences, but you must not change their order.***

1. We have no eggs. I cannot make an omelette.

   ____

2. Uncle James is an architect. He designs buildings.

   ____

3. Take a first-aid kit with you. Someone might have an accident.

   ____

4. He kept chopping at the trunk with his axe. The tree fell down.

   ____

5. The doorbell rang. Sally ran to the door.

   ____

6. The sun was shining. They stayed indoors all day.

   ____

 ISBN 978-81-8477-753-6

7. Jack forgot his passport. He could not get on the plane.

____

8. I searched my bedroom. I could not find my watch anywhere.

____

9. Alice felt sick. She had eaten too much.

____

10. Tom played the guitar. Billy played the drums.

____

 ISBN 978-81-8477-753-6

16 Punctuation: Commas and Semicolons

Grammar Help

Commas have many different uses in sentences.

- You put commas between items in a list. For example: *Please bring a picnic lunch**,** some money and a waterproof coat. There is no milk**,** orange juice**,** cola or lemonade in the fridge.* Note that you do not need to put a comma before **and** or **or**.
- You put a comma after a saying verb at the beginning of direct speech. For example: *Paul said**,** 'I am frightened.'*
- If the saying verb follows the spoken statement, you put a comma before the closing quotation mark, instead of a full stop. For example: *'I am frightened**,**' said Paul.* However, you do not replace question marks or exclamation marks with commas in this way.
- You usually put commas between two or more adjectives of quality used together before a noun. For example: *a* ***dull, cold, rainy*** *day.*
- You put a comma before **please** or a person's name at the end of a sentence. For example: *Open the door**, please**. May we go now**, Mr Jones**?*
- You also put a comma after **Yes, No** or a person's name at the beginning of a sentence. For example: ***No,*** *I have not read this book before.* ***Tom,*** *is this your football?*
- You sometimes put a comma after an introductory word, phrase or clause at the beginning of a sentence. This may be an adverb or an adverbial phrase (such as one used as a transitional device), a phrase containing a participle or a clause beginning with a conjunction. For example: ***Fortunately,*** *nobody noticed her mistake.* ***Stepping off the boat,*** *I slipped and fell into the water.* ***If you cannot answer one of the questions,*** *move on to the next.*
- You sometimes put a comma before extra information added to a sentence, such as a non-defining relative clause. For example: Mum had *lunch with Jane Smith**, an old schoolfriend**. The saucepan is made of aluminium**, which does not rust**.*
- If this extra information is in the middle of the sentence, you put another comma after it. *Mum met Jane Smith**, an old schoolfriend,** at the shopping mall. Aluminium**, which does not rust,** is used to make saucepans.*

 ISBN 978-81-8477-753-6

A ***Insert all the missing commas in this passage.***

Mary was doing her homework when she heard a crash and a scream. Looking out of the window she saw a man lying on the ground beside a fallen ladder. It was Joe Smith her next-door neighbour. She ran outside to help him.

'What happened Joe?' she asked. He replied 'I was cleaning my upstairs windows and the ladder slipped. I think I may have broken my leg. Can you call an ambulance for me please?' Mary returned to her house and spoke to her mother who was in the kitchen. 'Joe Smith has had an accident' she said.

While her mother phoned for an ambulance Mary went back outside to make Joe more comfortable. She took him a blanket a cushion for his head and a cool refreshing glass of water. About ten minutes later the ambulance arrived. They took Joe to the hospital to have his leg X-rayed.

Meanwhile Mary's mother phoned Joe's wife a nurse at the hospital to tell her what had happened. She said that she would go straight to the emergency department to see her husband.

B ***All these sentences contain mistakes involving commas. Rewrite them correctly on the lines below. You will need to move, add or remove at least one comma in each sentence.***

1. David asked 'Do you think it will rain today?'

___

2. The bookstore also sells newspapers, magazines, paper pens and cards.

___

3. The bride was wearing a long, white, dress.

___

 ISBN 978-81-8477-753-6

4. 'You have made several spelling mistakes.' said the teacher.

____

5. Please, do not walk on the grass.

____

6. I bought a ripe juicy melon, and some large, red apples.

____

7. The man who wrote this book, was at school with my father.

____

8. Neither Paul, nor his brother knew where their mother was.

____

9. Alice, is a polite well-behaved girl.

____

10 Wearing only his pyjamas he ran, out of the house.

____

11. The prize, a silver trophy will be given to the team, which answers the most questions, correctly.

____

12. However there was no phone number on the advertisement, in the newspaper.

____

C ***Write twelve sentences of your own. Each sentence must contain at least one comma. Your sentences should illustrate all the different uses of commas listed in the box at the beginning of this unit.***

1. ____
2. ____
3. ____
4. ____
5. ____
6. ____

 ISBN 978-81-8477-753-6

7. ______________________________

8. ______________________________

9. ______________________________

10. ______________________________

11. ______________________________

12. ______________________________

D ***Complete each sentence with a phrase or clause from the box, adding commas where necessary. Take care! Some of the sentences do not need commas.***

which you gave me	**where polar bears live**	**her favourite colour**
who needs it	**which cannot fly**	**members of the cat family**
our English teacher	**who wear glasses**	**which is bad for your teeth**
that were stolen	**a famous German composer**	**who said it was very good**

1. Leopards and tigers ______________________ use the markings on their bodies for camouflage.
2. The music is by Beethoven ______________________.
3. People ______________________ are either long-sighted or short-sighted.
4. The Arctic Ocean ______________________ is covered with ice.
5. You should not eat too much sugar ______________________.
6. There is enough food for everyone ______________________.
7. Mr Smith ______________________ comes from New York.
8. I showed my picture to Mum ______________________.
9. Penguins ______________________ use their flippers for swimming.
10. One of the rings ______________________ is very valuable.
11. Jane's new dress is red ______________________.
12. I bought a DVD with the money ______________________.

 ISBN 978-81-8477-753-6

Grammar Help

- You sometimes use a **semicolon** (;) instead of a comma to separate items in a list. You do this when the items are long and complex, especially if they contain commas of their own. For example: *The monster had hard, rough, scaly skin**;** large feet with sharp claws**;** a long tail that moved constantly from side to side**;** and, most terrifying of all, a huge mouth with several rows of teeth.*
- When you use semicolons in this way you usually put one before **and** or **or** near the end of the list. However, some lists containing semicolons do not need either of these conjunctions. For example: *Here are three easy ways to save water: turn off the tap while you brush your teeth**;** have a shower instead of a bath**;** use water from washing vegetables to water your garden.*

E ***Insert all the missing semicolons and commas in these sentences.***

1. You will need the following items: a large square piece of wood a box of nails some black paint and an assortment of tools including a saw and a hammer.
2. Mum bought carrots onions and tomatoes at the market bread and cakes at the baker's some meat at the butcher's and a bouquet of lovely sweet-smelling flowers for Grandma at the florist's.
3. I have invited ten people to my party: Carol my best friend four other friends from school two of my cousins Paul and Joe and Tom Kate and Sally who live next door.
4. If a fire starts in the building this is what you must do: sound the fire alarm leave by the nearest exit call the fire brigade wait at some distance from the building such as the far side of the car park.
5. We visited Buckingham Palace and the Tower of London on Monday the National Art Gallery the British Museum and Hyde Park on Tuesday and Covent Garden a busy shopping area on Wednesday.
6. A healthy diet contains fresh fruit and vegetables which are a good source of fibre protein which is found in meat fish eggs and milk and carbohydrates for energy.

 ISBN 978-81-8477-753-6

17 Punctuation: Hyphens, Dashes, Brackets and Ellipses

Grammar Help

- A **hyphen** is a short line that joins two or more words together to form a compound word, such as a compound noun, adjective or adverb. For example: *food-processor, sister-in-law; self-confident, well-behaved, ten-year-old, half-heartedly, self-consciously.*
- Not all compound nouns have hyphens. Some are written as one word or as two words, such as *toothbrush* and *fire alarm.* Some can be written with or without a hyphen. For example, you can write *cement-mixer* or *cement mixer.*
- You sometimes remove the hyphens from a compound adjective when you use it after the noun. For example: *This is a **well-written** essay. This essay is **well written**.*
- Some words have one or more letters attached at the beginning with a hyphen. For example: *e-commerce, co-ordinate, ex-president, eco-friendly, anti-aircraft.* This short group of letters is called a prefix. (Most prefixes are attached without a hyphen, such as the first two letters of ***im**possible, **un**happiness* or ***re**build.*)
- Hyphens are often used in printed text when a long word does not fit in the gap at the end of a line. The word is broken between two syllables, with a hyphen after the first part. For example, if there is no room for the full word ***important*** at the end of a line, you can write ***impor-*** in the gap and ***tant*** at the beginning of the next line. There must be at least two letters of the word on each line.

A ***Insert all the missing hyphens in this passage. You should add twelve hyphens altogether.***

Uncle Jack is my mother's brother in law. He is married to her sister, Aunt Julie. Uncle Jack has been a taxi driver for twenty five years. He loves his work and says that he would never want to do any other job. Sometimes it can be rather boring and frustrating, for example when he gets stuck in slow moving traffic during the rush hour. However, at other times it can be quite exciting.

 ISBN 978-81-8477-753-6

One day he stopped beside a bank so that his passenger could use the cash dispenser there. While he was waiting, a masked man carrying a gun ran out of the bank, knocking down a middle aged woman on the pavement, and raced off down the street. Uncle Jack called the police on his mobile phone, then he and his passenger helped the passer by who had been knocked down. Fortunately she was not badly hurt.

Aunt Julie is not so keen on her husband's job. Sometimes he works a sixteen hour day, which means that he does not see much of their children. They have a four year old son, Ali, and twin daughters who are just six months old. Ali likes riding around with his father. He wants to become a taxi driver as soon as he is old enough to take his driving test. Only fourteen years to wait!

B ***Fill in each blank with a compound word formed by joining a word from box A with a hyphen to a word from box B.***

A

self	long	ear	English	take	thirty
hair	ten	part	break	runner	cold

B

awaited	blooded	minute	up	speaking	in
confidence	time	off	dryer	piercing	six

1. This restaurant is popular with ________________ tourists.
2. Reptiles are ________________ animals.
3. Tom has more ________________ than his brother does.
4. There are ________________ students in my class.
5. The workers have a ________________ tea break during the morning.
6. There has been a ________________ at the supermarket.
7. The silence was broken by the ________________ sound of the siren.

 ISBN 978-81-8477-753-6

8. Please may I borrow your ________________?

9. The factory does not employ any ____________________ staff.

10. Will the ____________________ receive a prize too?

11. The ____________________ letter finally arrived.

12. The plane is now ready for ____________________.

C ***If you had to break these words at the end of a line, where would you put the hyphens? Draw a line between the letters where a hyphen could go. If there are two or more possible places, put a line in each one. The first three words have been done as examples.***

grace | ful	dif | fi | cult	cap | tain
sister	movement	winner
bathroom	incorrect	softly
happiness	useless	underneath
plastered	convention	signalling

Grammar Help

- A **dash** is a punctuation mark that looks like a long hyphen. You sometimes see a dash in printed text where a sentence is broken off before the end. For example: *'Good morning,' said one of the women, 'I am Kate Smith, and this is –' She stared at her companion, embarrassed to have forgotten her name.*
- A more common use of the dash is to add something that either explains what has gone before or indicates a new direction of thought. For example: *I did not buy the ring – it was far too expensive. We need some wood to burn – those broken chairs will do.*

D ***Combine these sentences in pairs to make eight longer sentences with a dash in the middle of each one. The first one has been done to help you.***

~~The fog was too thick.~~	He spilt cola on the new rug.
The car won't start.	Help yourselves to food and drink.
I wonder where she bought that dress.	It's time for lunch.

 ISBN 978-81-8477-753-6

Jane looks nice.

Do you have his phone number?

Sam was not at school today.

There's a nice restaurant near here.

There's plenty for everybody.

Mum is cross with my brother.

Peter might know the answer.

The battery must be flat.

He has a bad cold.

~~We could not see where we were going.~~

1. We could not see where we were going – the fog was too thick.
2. ______
3. ______
4. ______
5. ______
6. ______
7. ______
8. ______

Grammar Help

- You use **round brackets** (also called parentheses) in pairs around extra information added to a sentence. This additional material may be an explanation or a comment about the word or phrase it follows. For example: *Paris* **(***the capital of France***)** *is a city on the River Seine. A cricket pitch is 22 yards* **(***20.12 metres***)** *long. We had strawberries* **(***my favourite fruit***)** *for dessert.*
- You can also put round brackets around letters or numbers in a list. For example: *There are three ways of printing the document:* **(a)** *by clicking the printer icon on the computer screen,* **(b)** *by choosing 'Print' from the drop-down menu or* **(c)** *by pressing the 'Print' button on the printer.*

 ISBN 978-81-8477-753-6

E ***Insert the missing pairs of round brackets in these sentences.***

1. Carol Smith a girl in our class can swim ten lengths of the pool .
2. The book cost 540 rupees about six dollars .
3. They have four children two girls and two boys and numerous pets .
4. Mum's birthday 24 March falls on a Saturday this year .
5. I walked from Orchard Lane the street where I live to Castle Towers the apartment block where my grandparents live .
6. Use a ruler if you have one to draw a line down the middle of the page .
7. Nobody likes Mark Jones, a because he is a bully and b because he tells lies .
8. We saw a huge bird possibly an eagle swoop down from the sky .
9. Light enters your eyes through the pupils the dark holes in the middle .
10. Miss Lee gave me an A the highest mark for my essay on Captain Cook an 18th-century explorer .

F ***Rewrite these sentences, adding one of the phrases in the box in round brackets to each one.***

probably a ruby	**greenish-blue**	**large claws on their feet**
a Harry Potter DVD	**an African desert**	**a dark-coloured wood**
meat-eating	**energy from the sun**	**about 1.8 metres**
a famous actor		

1. I opened Paul's present last of all.

____

2. The water is heated by solar power.

____

3. The birds use their talons to seize their prey.

____

 ISBN 978-81-8477-753-6

4. The fabric is turquoise with white strips.

5. Alice met Brad Pitt while she was in New York.

6. Most of the furniture was made of mahogany.

7. My English cousin is six feet tall.

8. The ring had a large red stone surrounded by diamonds.

9. Carnivorous animals have sharp pointed teeth.

10. We watched a documentary about the Sahara.

Grammar Help

- **Ellipses** are a set of three dots used in place of missing words or letters. You can use them to shorten a quotation. For example: *Winston Churchill said, 'We shall fight on the beaches ... we shall never surrender.'*
- You can also use ellipses at the end of a sentence that is left incomplete. This may indicate that the speaker or writer is just thinking the missing words. For example: *I don't need another camera, but this one is such good value ...* (In this case, the ellipses could represent the words *that I am tempted to buy it.*) Alternatively, ellipses may indicate that the speaker or writer does not need to complete the statement. For example:
  As the saying goes, 'When the cat's away ...'.

 ISBN 978-81-8477-753-6

G ***Shorten the statements in quotation marks by rewriting them with ellipses in the place of a group of words. The first one has been done as an example.***

1. The writer said, 'People who commit such crimes should be locked away for life. They should never be released.'

   The writer said, 'People who commit such crimes ... should never be released.'

2. As someone once said, 'Money can solve many problems but it cannot make you happy.'

3. The saying 'Don't count your chickens before they're hatched' comes to mind.

4. The president said, 'This new resort, which has created thousands of jobs for local people, will restore prosperity to the region.'

5. Remember the saying 'Sticks and stones may break your bones but words can never hurt you' and ignore their cruel remarks.

6. The policeman said, 'The accident was caused by the driver's carelessness and could have been prevented.'

 ISBN 978-81-8477-753-6

18 Phrases, Clauses and Sentences

Grammar Help

A **phrase** is a group of words that are used together to do the work of a particular word class.

- A **noun phrase** consists of a noun or pronoun with other words (such as articles, adjectives or phrases) that tell you more about it. For example: *a* ***book****; this* ***house****; my new* ***shoes****; two very small* ***pictures****; the* ***people*** *in the queue;* ***something*** *unusual.*
- A long noun phrase sometimes contains two or more shorter noun phrases. For example, the long noun phrase ***the people in the queue*** contains the shorter noun phrases *the people* and *the queue.*
- Noun phrases nearly always do the work of a noun, but they can occasionally do the work of an adverb instead. For example: *We are moving house* ***next month****. You are not doing it* ***the right way****.*
- As you learnt in Unit 12, a **prepositional phrase** is a group of words beginning with a preposition. For example: ***with*** *long hair;* ***over*** *the fence;* ***in*** *bed;* ***to*** *my sister.*
- Prepositional phrases can be used as adjectival phrases. For example: *I saw a girl* ***with long hair****.* (Notice that this adjectival phrase is also part of the noun phrase ***a girl with long hair****.*)
- Another kind of **adjectival phrase** consists of an adverb followed by an adjective or participle. For example: *more difficult; extremely cold; neatly written.*
- As you learnt in Unit 10, prepositional phrases can also be used as adverbial phrases. For example: *The horse jumped* ***over the fence****.*
- In that unit you learnt about other kinds of **adverbial phrases** as well. For example: *next week; two years ago; very badly; out there.*

A ***Underline all the noun phrases in these sentences. Some phrases may be underlined twice if they are also part of a longer noun phrase.***

For example: The grapes on these vines are used to make red wine.

1. Joe walked to school with his best friend.
2. There is nothing interesting on television today.
3. A man with a bad cough was sitting behind me on the bus.
4. A cheetah can run faster than any other animal.

 ISBN 978-81-8477-753-6

5. You will find the dictionary on the top shelf of the bookcase.
6. A very tall woman was standing behind the counter.
7. Sally gave her sister a box of chocolates for her birthday.
8. The person responsible must be punished for this terrible crime.
9. Mum put a mat under the hot dish.
10. Tom lay on his back on the grass looking up at the fluffy white clouds in the sky.
11. Last year we went to England for three weeks.
12. Mary told me a secret and I promised not to tell anyone else.

B ***Fill in each blank in this passage with a phrase from the box.***

at her watch	**their friends and relatives**	**hand in hand**
all alone	**in a business suit**	**extremely slowly**
one by one	**a few minutes later**	**his mobile phone**
very long	**an empty parking space**	**to the station**

A young man ______________________ carrying a large suitcase stepped off the train. He walked slowly along the platform, looking for a familiar face among the people who had come to meet ______________________. He had phoned his wife the previous evening to tell her which train he was arriving on, and she had promised to come and pick him up. Where was she?

The man sat down on a seat as ______________________ his fellow-passengers left the station. Soon he was ______________________, feeling rather self-conscious. He checked ______________________ but there were no messages for him.

 ISBN 978-81-8477-753-6

Meanwhile, on the busy street leading ______________________, his wife was sitting in a ______________________ traffic jam looking anxiously ______________________. She did not have far to go, but the traffic was moving ______________________. Having spotted ______________________ beside a row of shops, she decided to leave the car there and run the rest of the way.

______________________ she and her husband were hugging each other on the station platform. He was really pleased to see her, not only because he had been away for a week, but also because he had been so worried when she was not there to greet him. They walked back to the parked car ______________________.

C ***Now list sixteen of the phrases from the passage in B under the headings below. You can include some phrases that were already in the text as well as some of those you have added. Do not list any phrase twice.***

Noun phrases	**Adjectival phrases**
______________________	______________________
______________________	______________________
______________________	______________________
______________________	______________________

Adverbial phrases	**Prepositional phrases**
______________________	______________________
______________________	______________________
______________________	______________________
______________________	______________________

 ISBN 978-81-8477-753-6

Grammar Help

A **clause** is a part of a sentence that contains a verb (together with other words such as its subject, its object and/or any adverbial phrases that go with it). For example, the sentence, '*I have lost the book that you gave me for my birthday*' contains two clauses: *I have lost the book* and *that you gave me for my birthday*. The sentence, '*She screamed but nobody heard her*' also contains two clauses: '*She screamed*' and '*nobody heard her*.'

- A **main clause** can stand alone as a sentence, whereas a **subordinate clause** cannot. For example, in the sentence, '*Joe went to bed early because he felt tired*,' the main clause is '*Joe went to bed early*' and '*because he felt tired*' is a subordinate clause. You will learn more about main clauses and subordinate clauses in Unit 19.
- A **relative clause** is a type of subordinate clause. You learnt about relative clauses in Unit 3. For example: *I have lost the book* ***that you gave me for my birthday***. *Mr Jones,* ***who lives next door****, is a car mechanic.*
- The verb in a clause does not always have a subject. For example: ***Ring the bell*** *if you need any help. Sally picked up the envelope and* ***opened it****. Mr Jones,* ***who lives next door****, is a car mechanic.*

D ***Look at the words in bold print in these sentences. If they make up a phrase, write P in the brackets. If they make up a clause, write C.***

1. My favourite programme is on TV **this afternoon**. ( )
2. **Jack failed the test** because he made a lot of mistakes. ( )
3. The roof leaks **when it rains**. ( )
4. The box **in the corner** contains old newspapers and magazines. ( )
5. I took a photo of **a bird with red and green feathers**. ( )
6. Alice went into her bedroom and **closed the door**. ( )
7. **The name of the ship** is painted on the side. ( )
8. **Put up your hand** if you know the answer. ( )
9. The boy **who won** is a friend of my brother's. ( )
10. You can find **the answers to all these questions** on the Internet. ( )

 ISBN 978-81-8477-753-6

Grammar Help

- A **sentence** is a group of words that makes a statement (a **declarative** sentence), asks a question (an **interrogative** sentence), gives a command (an **imperative** sentence) or makes an exclamation (an **exclamatory** sentence). All sentences begin with a capital letter and end with a full stop, question mark or exclamation mark. For example: *The water is too cold. Why is Tom laughing? Put your books away. What a mess!*
- Most sentences contain a subject and a verb. However, imperative sentences have no subject and short exclamatory sentences often do not have a subject or a verb. For example: *Put your books away.* (imperative). *What a mess!* (exclamatory).
- A **simple sentence** contains a single clause. For example: *I took off my jacket.* A **compound sentence** contains two main clauses linked by a co-ordinating conjunction. For example: *I took off my jacket and hung it on a peg.* A **complex sentence** contains a main clause and a subordinate clause.
  For example: *I took off my jacket because I was too hot.* You will learn more about compound and complex sentences in Unit 20.

E ***Write sentences of your own containing the given phrase or clause. Try to include some interrogative and imperative sentences as well as declarative ones.***

1. (a book about dinosaurs) ____________________
2. (who work hard) ____________________
3. (at the zoo) ____________________
4. (when we left) ____________________
5. (in the country) ____________________
6. (as Mary can) ____________________
7. (rather foolishly) ____________________
8. (bicycles have two wheels) ____________________
9. (these pictures) ____________________
10. (go away) ____________________

 ISBN 978-81-8477-753-6

19 Main Clauses and Subordinate Clauses

Grammar Help

There are two types of clauses: main clauses and subordinate clauses. Relative clauses are a type of subordinate clause.

- All sentences (except exclamatory ones) must contain a **main clause**. The clause can stand alone as a simple sentence. For example: ***I found the key.***
- A **subordinate clause** cannot stand alone. It begins with a subordinating conjunction (such as **when**, **because**, **if**) or a relative pronoun (such as **that, which, who**) and it is used with a main clause to form a sentence. For example: *I found the key* ***while I was tidying the room***. *I found the key* ***that I was looking for***. ***If the phone rings,*** *do not answer it. The man* ***who spoke to me*** *had grey hair and glasses.*
- Some sentences contain two main clauses linked by one of the co-ordinating conjunctions **and**, **or**, **but** or **so**. For example: ***I found the key*** *but* ***it did not fit in the lock.*** You sometimes omit the subject of the second clause if it is the same as the first. For example: ***I found the key*** *and* ***unlocked the door.***

A ***Look at the words in bold print in these sentences. If they make up a main clause, write M in the brackets. If they make up a subordinate clause, write S.***

1. Did you see the queen **while you were in England**? ( )
2. **Jane pointed to the boy** who had hit her. ( )
3. The monkey grabbed the banana and **ran away with it**. ( )
4. Here is a list of all the things **that you will need**. ( )
5. **Paul likes drawing pictures** but he hates writing stories. ( )
6. If you have toothache, **you should go to the dentist**. ( )
7. **When Grandpa was young**, there were no computers or mobile phones. ( )
8. Tom overslept so **he was late for school**. ( )
9. **Should I heat the pie** or would you prefer to eat it cold? ( )
10. Alice checked her test paper for mistakes **before she handed it in**. ( )
11. I went to the beach with my friend, **whose brother is a lifeguard there**. ( )

 ISBN 978-81-8477-753-6

12. **Please switch off the computer** after you have finished using it. ( )
13. The person **who wrote this poem** had a good sense of humour. ( )
14. Paul is unpopular **because he is a bully**. ( )
15. Carol passed the English test but **failed the maths test.** ( )
16. **As soon as I saw the boy** I knew he must be your brother. ( )

B ***Draw lines to link each main clause with a suitable subordinate clause.***

1. Dad cleaned the house •	• that they grow.
2. I showed my friend the photos •	• he cannot speak English.
3. When the apples are ripe •	• who could do magic tricks.
4. This is the boy •	• they were each given a reward.
5. If you eat too much •	• unless I am going to be late.
6. Mary had a cousin •	• so that she could see better.
7. Take some money with you •	• in case you need to get a taxi home.
8. Although Ali lives in England •	• whose bicycle has been stolen.
9. Sue switched on the lamp •	• you will get fat.
10. Because the children had done well •	• while Mum was at the shops.
11. Farmers sell most of the crops •	• that I had taken.
12. I shall not phone you •	• we shall pick them.

Grammar Help

- A subordinate clause beginning with a conjunction usually comes after the main clause, but it can sometimes come before it. For example: *You will get wet* ***if it rains. If it rains*** *you will get wet.*
- You sometimes put a comma after a subordinate clause at the beginning of a sentence, especially if it is long or complicated. For example: ***Because none of the guests was feeling very hungry,*** *there was a lot of food left over.*

 ISBN 978-81-8477-753-6

- A relative clause can come after the main clause or in the middle of it, depending on the position of the noun phrase it refers to. For example: *Nobody liked the picture* ***which I drew****. The picture* ***which I drew*** *was not very good.*
- You always use commas with non-defining relative clauses (those containing additional information that is not essential). For example: *This necklace****, which is made of gold,*** *is very valuable. I lent my pen to Sally****, who had lost hers****.*
- You never use commas with defining relative clauses (those containing essential information). For example: *People* ***who tell lies*** *should be punished. Tom bought a new bike with the money* ***that he earned****.*

C ***Underline all the subordinate clauses in this passage. Take care to underline the complete clause.***

There was a serious accident on the expressway yesterday morning. The road was very busy because many people were on their way to work. There was also a lot of rainwater on the road, which made the surface slippery. A truck had a puncture and stopped suddenly. The car behind it, which was going too fast, crashed into it. When other drivers saw this, some of them slowed down. However, those who were not paying enough attention drove straight into the back of the vehicles in front of them. There was a huge pile-up.

The driver of the truck, who was unhurt, phoned the emergency services. As soon as they received the call they sent the police and an ambulance to the scene. They also sent a fire engine in case any of the vehicles caught fire. The police closed the expressway so that there would be no further collisions. Meanwhile, the ambulance crew attended to the people who were trapped in their cars. Miraculously, nobody was very badly hurt.

 ISBN 978-81-8477-753-6

D ***Rewrite these sentences, adding a subordinate clause from the box to each one. You should put at least two of the subordinate clauses at the beginning of the new sentences and at least two in the middle. Add commas where appropriate or necessary.***

if you don't know the correct spelling	**before he goes to school**
whose names are Paul and Tom	**as I was getting dressed**
while you are at the supermarket	**which live on the farm**
that she had found	**who does not have a car**
because it was very untidy	**which is a long way from here**

1. David does an hour's piano practice.

 ____

2. Our principal comes to school by bus.

 ____

3. Look up the word in a dictionary.

 ____

4. My grandparents live in Karachi.

 ____

5. Mr Smith has two sons.

 ____

6. Nobody could read the writing.

 ____

7. I noticed a hole in one of my socks.

 ____

8. Sally gave the ball to her brother.

 ____

9. Most of the animals eat grass or hay.

 ____

10. Please buy me some shampoo.

 ____

 ISBN 978-81-8477-753-6

E ***Make sentences of your own by adding an appropriate main clause at the beginning. You can add a comma before a relative clause if you need to.***

1. ______________________________ unless you speak more loudly.
2. ______________________________ so I tiptoed out of the room.
3. ______________________________ who flies a plane.
4. ______________________________ and it began to rain.
5. ______________________________ which are good for you.
6. ______________________________ when the dog started barking.
7. ______________________________ but he did not have enough money.
8. ______________________________ whose picture won first prize.
9. ______________________________ although his feet were sore.
10. ______________________________ or you can sleep on the sofa.
11. ______________________________ because she is allergic to it.
12. ______________________________ that we had caught.
13. ______________________________ but she did not see me.
14. ______________________________ before you eat it.
15. ______________________________ so they ran away.
16. ______________________________ who has four young children.

 ISBN 978-81-8477-753-6

20 Simple, Compound and Complex Sentences

Grammar Help

- A **simple sentence** contains only one clause, no matter how long it is. For example: *It is raining. A waiter with a tray of glasses in his hands walked slowly and carefully up the stairs.*
- A **compound sentence** contains two main clauses linked by one of the co-ordinating conjunctions **and**, **or**, **but** or **so**. For example: *I washed the towel* ***and*** *hung it up to dry. Colin told a joke* ***but*** *nobody laughed.*
- A **complex sentence** contains a main clause and a subordinate clause. The subordinate clause may begin with a subordinating conjunction and come before or after the main clause. For example: *I could not see very far* ***because it was foggy. If you win the race,*** *you will receive a medal.* Alternatively, it may begin with a relative pronoun and come in the middle or at the end of the main clause. For example: *J. K. Rowling,* ***who wrote the Harry Potter books,*** *studied French at university. I have spent all the money* ***that you gave me.***

A ***This passage contains sentences of all three types. Write S in the brackets at the end of the simple sentences. Write Cd at the end of the compound sentences. Write Cx at the end of the complex sentences.***

There is a volcano in the middle of the island ( ). It has not erupted for many years but it is still active ( ). In other words, it could erupt again at any time ( ). The people who live on the island are in constant danger ( ). If the volcano erupts, they might be killed ( ). They could be burnt by the hot lava or they could be buried under the volcanic debris ( ). Even if they survived the eruption themselves, their houses might be destroyed ( ).

However, most of them are not afraid ( ). Some were young children when the volcano last erupted ( ). These people remember the heat and

 ISBN 978-81-8477-753-6

dust that filled the air (   ). They survived that eruption so they do not fear the next one (   ). They simply get on with their lives and ignore the danger in their midst (   ).

B ***Rewrite each of these pairs of simple sentences as a compound or complex sentence. Use a different conjunction or relative pronoun each time. The first one has been done as an example.***

1. This car is quite cheap to run. It uses less fuel than our old one.

   This car, which uses less fuel than our old one, is quite cheap to run.

2. Anna closed the window. Then she drew the curtains.

   ____

3. The front tyre of my bicycle was flat. I pumped it up.

   ____

4. Bring a swimsuit. We may go swimming.

   ____

5. The car stopped. A smartly dressed man got out.

   ____

6. Uncle Jack is afraid of flying. He never travels by air.

   ____

7. Mrs Lee said I should have an anti-influenza injection. She is a nurse.

   ____

8. Tom pushed the door. It did not open.

   ____

9. Mary entered the competition. She did not think she had much chance of winning it.

   ____

10. Should I glue the pieces together? Should I use sticky tape instead?

    ____

 ISBN 978-81-8477-753-6

11. David's alarm clock went off. He leapt out of bed.

____

12. Mr and Mrs Jones are moving to a smaller house. Their children have left home.

____

C ***Add a conjunction and a second main clause of your own to make each of these simple sentences into a compound sentence. You should use each of the four co-ordinating conjunctions (and, or, but, so) at least twice.***

1. The thief ran out of the shop ______________________.
2. The pianist played a few wrong notes ______________________.
3. They might be held up in traffic ______________________.
4. The baby was crying ______________________.
5. At the weekend we visit our grandparents ______________________.
6. Alice washed her hair ______________________.
7. Paul was struggling with his homework ______________________.
8. I would like to be a doctor ______________________.
9. Carol sold her old camera ______________________.
10. John and Sue are going to a concert ______________________.
11. Sally liked the black shoes best ______________________.
12. You can phone the company ______________________.

D ***Rewrite these sentences, adding a clause of your own to make them into complex sentences. You should put some of the clauses at the beginning, some in the middle and some at the end.***

1. Mum was worried.

____

2. I stayed till the end of the party.

____

3. You will not pass your exam.

____

 ISBN 978-81-8477-753-6

4. The battery is fully charged.

___

5. The photos have not come out very well.

___

6. You should tell your teacher or your parents.

___

7. Joe has earned a lot of money.

___

8. This letter is from Peter.

___

9. I noticed that a new bookstore had opened.

___

10. The old prison has been converted into luxury apartments.

___

11. Grandpa felt much better.

___

12. We shall go over this topic again in the next lesson.

___

E ***Answer each question with a full sentence of the type shown in brackets. The first one has been done as an example.***

1. When did Mum make this cake?

   (**complex**) She made it while we were at school.

2. Do you live in a house or a flat?

   (**simple**) ___

3. What is a saw?

   (**complex**) ___

4. How should I cook the chicken?

   (**compound**) ___

 ISBN 978-81-8477-753-6

5. When does the show start?

   (**simple**) ______________________________

6. What did you do after you got up this morning?

   (**compound**) ______________________________

7. Why are you laughing?

   (**complex**) ______________________________

8. What is an orphan?

   (**complex**) ______________________________

9. Why isn't Michael coming to the swimming pool with us?

   (**compound**) ______________________________

10. How many legs does a spider have?

    (**simple**) ______________________________

11. Where should I put these books?

    (**simple**) ______________________________

12. Have you told Grandma your good news yet?

    (**compound**) ______________________________

 ISBN 978-81-8477-753-6

21 Active and Passive Voice

Grammar Help

- In the active voice, the subject of the verb does the action. For example: *The baker makes the bread.* In the passive voice, the subject of the verb receives the action. For example: *The bread is made by the baker.* The object of the active verb becomes the subject of the passive verb.
- The subject of the passive verb is sometimes mentioned in the passive sentence, as above. However, some passive sentences do not mention the doer of the action, if this person or thing is unknown, unimportant or obvious. For example: *My ring has been stolen. This room is mainly used for meetings. The building was burnt to the ground.*
- A passive verb is made up of the helping verb **be** + the past participle of the main verb. Here is a table of active verbs and their passive equivalents:

	ACTIVE	**PASSIVE**
present tense	*take/takes*	*am/is/are taken*
past tense	*took*	*was/were taken*
present continuous	*am/is/are taking*	*am/is/are being taken*
past continuous	*was/were taking*	*was/were being taken*
present perfect	*has/have taken*	*has/have been taken*
past perfect	*had taken*	*had been taken*
future	*will/shall take*	*will/shall be taken*
with *do/does*	*do/does not take*	*am/is/are not taken*
with *did*	*did not take*	*was/were not taken*
with modal verb	*can/must/etc take*	*can/must/etc be taken*

 ISBN 978-81-8477-753-6

A ***Are these verbs in the active or passive voice, and what tense are they in? Write active or passive in the middle column and the correct tense name in the right-hand column.***

	VERB	VOICE	TENSE
1.	were being fed	______	______
2.	have shown	______	______
3.	are playing	______	______
4.	had been built	______	______
5.	was wearing	______	______
6.	were awarded	______	______
7.	had seen	______	______
8.	is being picked	______	______
9.	are allowed	______	______
10.	will be	______	______

B ***Now use each of these verbs in a sentence of your own. You can make the verb negative or interrogative, if you like.***

1. ______
2. ______
3. ______
4. ______
5. ______
6. ______
7. ______
8. ______
9. ______
10. ______

 ISBN 978-81-8477-753-6

C ***Change these sentences from the active voice to the passive voice. Do not include the subject of the active verb in the passive sentence unless it is necessary to do so.***

1. My grandparents planted this tree.

   ____

2. We do not grow wheat on this farm.

   ____

3. Did anyone tell you what to do?

   ____

4. You can wear it as a scarf or as a hood.

   ____

5. A large black dog was chasing the cat.

   ____

6. Sally and Tom have not invited me to their wedding.

   ____

7. All Alice's friends had signed her get-well card.

   ____

8. I shall give you your test results tomorrow.

   ____

D ***Change these sentences from the passive voice to the active voice. You will need to supply an appropriate subject for the active verb if it is not given in the passive sentence.***

1. The people inside the store are constantly being filmed by the security cameras.

   ____

2. School uniform is not worn at this school.

   ____

3. The judges were impressed by Colin's performance.

   ____

 ISBN 978-81-8477-753-6

4. The thief has been arrested.

____

5. Several houses had been swept away by the flood.

____

6. The costumes for the play will be made by Mrs Green.

____

7. Fresh fruit and vegetables can be bought at the market.

____

8. This scrap paper is not wanted.

____

E ***Fill in each blank with a verb from the box in an appropriate tense of the active or passive voice.***

use	sell	treat	repair	wash
like	forget	look	sail	hurt

1. Paul told the teacher that he ____________ to do his homework.
2. We shall have no access to the Internet while the computer ____________.
3. Hyphens ____________ to join words together.
4. You ____________ yourself if you fall.
5. These jeans ____________ so often that their colour has faded.
6. We ____________ across the lake when the storm broke.
7. Nobody ____________ to be accused of lying.
8. The people injured in the accident ____________ at a nearby hospital.
9. We ____________ after our neighbours' pets while they are on holiday.
10. All the tickets ____________ by the time we arrived.

 ISBN 978-81-8477-753-6

22 Direct and Indirect Speech

Grammar Help

When you write a narrative you can use direct speech or indirect speech, or a mixture of the two, for the things that people say to each other.

- **Direct speech** gives someone's exact words inside quotation marks. The saying verb comes outside the quotation marks. For example: *Mr Lee announced, 'I am leaving at the end of term.' 'Did you enjoy the show, Mary?' I asked. 'Stop writing,' said the teacher, 'and look at the board.'* When the saying verb is in the middle or at the end, you can put the subject after the verb if it is not a personal pronoun. This is called inverting the subject and verb.
- **Indirect speech** has no quotation marks and usually does not give the person's exact words. For example: *Mr Lee announced that he was leaving at the end of term. I asked Mary if she had enjoyed the show. The teacher told the class to stop writing and look at the board.*
- When you change direct speech to indirect speech, you often have to change the tenses of verbs (from present to past, or past to past perfect), pronouns and determiners, time words (e.g. **yesterday → the day before**) and some other words. For example: *'**We are** moving house **next week**,' they said. → They said that **they were** moving house **the following week**.*
- When you change a declarative sentence to indirect speech, you often put **that** after the saying verb. For example: *'I am tired,' complained Jack. → Jack complained **that** he was tired.* However, you can omit **that** after **said**. For example: *Jack said he was tired.*
- When you change an interrogative sentence that does not begin with a question word to indirect speech, you put **if** or **whether** after the saying verb. For example: *'Is it raining?' asked Sally. → Sally asked **if** it was raining.*
- When you change an imperative sentence to indirect speech, you change the imperative verb to a **to**-infinitive. You often have to change the saying verb to **tell**, **ask** or something similar. For example: *'Sit down, children,' said the principal. → The principal told the children to sit down. I said to Mary, 'Please do not touch the model.' → I asked Mary not to touch the model.*

A ***Change these sentences from indirect speech to direct speech, putting the saying verb in the middle of four of the sentences and at the end of the other four. You should invert the subject and verb wherever it is correct to do so.***

1. I asked them what they were laughing at.

 ISBN 978-81-8477-753-6

2. Mum said she could not make any bread because she had no flour.

3. Sally said that she had last seen her brother two weeks earlier.

4. The policeman asked us if we had seen anything suspicious or heard any strange noises.

5. The guide told us not to stand too close to the edge.

6. He said that his father was a doctor and his mother was a teacher.

7. The captain told me to go and lie down in my cabin if I felt seasick.

8. Aunt Jane said she would phone us as soon as she got off the train.

B ***Change these sentences from direct speech to indirect speech. Use a different saying verb in each of your new sentences.***

1. The man at the door said to us, 'Take off your muddy boots!'

2. 'I shall mend your bike tomorrow,' said Dad.

3. 'Is the picture in the window for sale?' asked the customer.

4. 'Do not go out until you feel better,' the doctor said to Grandma.

5. 'When did the accident happen?' asked the reporter.

 ISBN 978-81-8477-753-6

6. 'The train to Springfield,' the station master said to me, 'does not stop here.'

___

___

7. 'Help yourselves, everyone,' said our hostess.

___

8. 'The children cannot understand what I am saying,' said Miss Jones, 'because they do not speak English.'

___

___

C ***On a sheet of paper, rewrite this dialogue as a narrative with a mixture of direct and indirect speech.***

Kate: What are you doing, Dad?

Dad: I'm making your mother a jewellery box for her birthday. It's a surprise, so don't tell her about it.

Kate: Can I do anything to help?

Dad: Not really, but you can watch me if you like.

Kate: Thank you. What is the name of that tool you are using?

Dad: It is called a fretsaw.

Kate: Are you going to paint the box when you have finished it?

Dad: Probably.

Kate: What colour will you paint it?

Dad: I have not decided yet.

Kate: Am I annoying you with all my questions?

Dad: Yes. Please go away and leave me alone.

 ISBN 978-81-8477-753-6

Unit 1: Concrete Nouns and Abstract Nouns

A CONCRETE: apples, baker, eagle, flour, gate, kite, men, mountain, oil, ruler
ABSTRACT: coolness, danger, hours, hunger, life, love, patience, speed, trouble, work

Possible answers:

Concrete nouns:

1. There are three apples in the bowl.
2. A baker makes bread and cakes.
3. We watched an eagle flying overhead.
4. I do not have enough flour to make a loaf.
5. Jane forgot to shut the gate.
6. Paul likes to fly his kite on a windy day.
7. The men are digging a hole in the road.
8. The top of the mountain is covered with snow.
9. Dad put some oil on the squeaky hinge.
10. I drew a straight line with my ruler.

Abstract nouns:

1. The coolness of the water was very refreshing.
2. The children did not realize that they were in danger.
3. It takes two hours to get to the airport from here.
4. The animals probably died of hunger.
5. Uncle Paul has spent most of his life at sea.
6. Mothers show their love in many different ways.
7. You need a lot of patience to be a teacher.
8. This device can measure the speed of a moving vehicle.
9. I don't want to get into trouble with my teacher.
10. Mrs Jones praised us for our hard work.

B

1. Some people find it hard to make decisions.
2. The boys were riding their bicycles.
3. A lovely smell was coming from the kitchen.
4. We do not have enough time to finish this task.
5. They carried the piano with difficulty.
6. You should show more respect to your parents.
7. I had a very strange dream last night.
8. The woman took a key out of her pocket.
9. The departure of the train was delayed by twenty minutes.
10. She bought a can of cola at the shop.

C

1. gratitude	2. praise
3. terror	4. confidence
5. courage	6. advice
7. anxiety	8. regret
9. help	10. sorrow

D airport (CC), land (CU), meeting (AC), people (CC), jobs (AC), unemployment (AU), travel (AU), idea (AC), noise (AU), traffic (CU)

E *Possible answers:*

1. This is a very easy exercise.
   You should take more exercise.
2. There is a hair in my soup.
   Jane has long black hair.
3. The T-shirts come in three sizes: small, medium and large.
   They were amazed at the size of the animal.
4. The principal's desk is always littered with papers.
   The printer has run out of paper.
5. The man said he could read people's thoughts.
   My teacher told me to put more thought into my writing.
6. Joe had an unpleasant surprise when he opened the box.
   She gasped with surprise when they told her she had won.
7. Iron, lead and copper are metals.
   The window frames were made of metal.
8. There have been several accidents at this junction.
   I deleted the computer file by accident.
9. Sally found a smooth white stone on the beach.
   The ground was as hard as stone.
10. Dad has caught a fish.
    Fish is better for you than red meat is.

F

1. warmth	2. honesty
3. freedom	4. impression
5. performance	6. carelessness
7. amazement	8. preference
9. loyalty	10. formation

G

1. naughtiness	2. education
3. activity	4. treatment
5. presence	6. delivery
7. relevance	8. conclusion
9. Loneliness	10. insurance

H

1. existence	2. ability
3. consideration	4. difference
5. persuasion	6. cruelty
7. amusement	8. foolishness
9. disapproval	10. expansion

Unit 2: Reflexive and Emphatic Pronouns

A

1. himself	2. itself
3. yourselves	4. myself
5. herself	6. ourselves
7. yourself	8. himself
9. ourselves	10. themselves

B

1. at herself
2. with myself
3. of himself
4. to herself
5. among yourselves
6. by himself
7. over myself
8. for themselves
9. about yourself
10. between ourselves

C

1. you	2. myself
3. herself	4. us
5. yourselves	6. I
7. himself	8. themselves
9. her	10. itself

D

1. R	2. R	3. E
4. R	5. E	6. E
7. R	8. E	9. R
10. E		

E

1. Carol and I had to do most of the work **ourselves**.
2. The letter was not from the queen **herself**, but from one of her ladies-in-waiting.
3. These buildings are older than the farmhouse **itself**.
4. I **myself** do not believe in ghosts. *Or* I do not believe in ghosts **myself**.
5. Did you make these cakes **yourselves**?
6. The festival **itself** takes place tomorrow.
7. Give the letter to Dr Green **himself**.
8. We did not see the statues **themselves**, just pictures of them.
9. You must pay for the ticket **yourself**. *Or* You **yourself** must pay for the ticket.
10. The singer **herself** was good but the rest of the group were awful.

F herself, himself, himself, herself, themselves, themselves, herself, itself, themselves, myself, yourself, yourselves

G *Possible answers:*

1. She considers herself a good cook.
2. The comedian himself did not laugh at the joke.
3. It was so noisy that we couldn't hear ourselves speak.
4. If you can't move the piano yourselves, Jack will help you.
5. I went home by myself.

 ISBN 978-81-8477-753-6

6. Each animal has its own way of protecting itself from predators.
7. Did you take this photo yourself?
8. People who have little money themselves cannot give generously to others.

Unit 3: Relative Pronouns

A 1. which 2. who 3. which
4. which 5. who 6. who
7. which 8. who 9. which
10. who

B 1. who have university degrees
2. that are not addressed to you
3. which we throw away
4. who broke the window
5. which I need
6. who need it most
7. that Jane saw
8. which Dad gave her
9. who fixed the roof
10. that you have made

C *Possible answers:*
1. An architect is a person who designs buildings.
2. An elephant is an animal that has a long trunk.
3. Ink is a liquid which is used for writing and printing.
4. A dictionary is a book that lists words and their meanings.
5. A liar is someone who does not tell the truth.
6. An emperor is a man who rules an empire.
7. A shark is a fish that lives in the sea.
8. A doctor is a person who treats the sick.
9. A waitress is a woman who works in a restaurant.
10. Rice is a plant which grows in hot countries.

D 1. We visited Paris, which is the capital of France.
3. My father, who speaks very good English, translated the notice.
7. Sally washed her hands, which were dirty, and combed her hair.
8. Mr Brown, who is our science teacher, explained how computers work.
10. The film stars Brad Pitt, who is my favourite actor.

E 2. Sally helped the boy, who thanked her.
3. I have lost my favourite necklace, which was a present from my aunt.
4. Dad took his car, which needed servicing, to the garage.
5. We gave some food to the children, who looked hungry.
6. Tom, who is afraid of heights, would not climb the ladder.
7. They stayed at the Grand Hotel, which is in the town centre.
8. Our neighbour, who likes animals, offered to look after our pets.
9. The Nile, which is in Africa, is the longest river in the world.
10. I am going to visit my grandmother, who is in hospital.

F 2. Dad left his car with the mechanic, who fixed it.
3. This ring, which is made of gold, belonged to my grandmother.
4. The girl opened the door, which was not locked.
5. The twins, who look exactly the same, enjoy confusing people.
6. Mr and Mrs Brown, who have no children, let us play in their garden.
7. During the night we saw several owls, which are nocturnal birds.
8. Uncle Joe, who is a strong swimmer, tried to rescue the boy.
9. My sister called her baby David, which was our grandfather's name.
10. I showed the rash to my uncle, who is a doctor.

G *Possible answers:*
1. Thank you very much for the birthday card that you sent me.
2. Joe, who has a broken ankle, will not be able to play in the match.
3. Spiders, which have eight legs, are not insects.
4. The singer bowed to the audience, who clapped and cheered.
5. Please pass me the screwdriver which is on the table.
6. The cheese that I bought yesterday has gone mouldy.
7. People who eat too much risk putting on weight.
8. Do you know the woman who lives in that house?
9. I gave my parents my school report, which was not very good.
10. Police officers and firefighters, who do dangerous work, deserve higher pay.

H A thief stole Grandma's handbag, which contained a lot of money, as she was walking home from the bank. She went to the police station and reported the theft to the officer who was standing behind the desk. The officer asked her to describe the man who had robbed her.

'He had long dark hair which looked as if it hadn't been washed for weeks,' said Grandma, 'and the jeans that he was wearing had holes in the knees.' She added that the man had a distinctive tattoo, which looked like a lizard, on his right arm.

'From that description,' said the officer, 'I think I know who the thief might be. It sounds like Joe Green, who has committed many similar crimes in the past.'

He showed Grandma a book that contained photos of various criminals and asked her which of the photos looked most like the thief. The pictures did not have names under them, but Grandma immediately pointed to the one of Joe Green. 'That is the man!' she said.

I which contained a lot of money
who was standing behind the desk
who had robbed her
which looked as if it hadn't been washed for weeks
that he was wearing
which looked like a lizard
who has committed many similar crimes in the past
that contained photos of various criminals

Unit 4: Linking Verbs

A 1. became 2. grew
3. sounded 4. was
5. seemed 6. went
7. got 8. felt
9. smelt 10. looked

B *Possible answers:*
1. a teacher 2. bitter
3. anxious 4. cloudy
5. a butterfly 6. happier
7. dark 8. very colourful
9. upset 10. hoarse

C 1. L, A 2. A, A 3. A, L
4. A, L 5. L, L 6. L, A
7. A, A 8. L, A 9. A, L
10. L, L

D *Possible answers:*
1. The cat's fur felt soft and smooth.
2. The berries turn red when they ripen.
3. David became the new captain of the football team.
4. I am getting tired of your impudence.
5. The air smelt fresh after the rain.
6. Tom didn't look very well.
7. The journey seemed longer than usual because I had nobody to talk to.
8. Owls are my favourite birds.
9. Our voices sound different to us when we hear them in a video.
10. The fruit tasted sweeter than I had expected it to.

E *Possible answers:*
1. You turn this handle to operate the machine.
2. I got a good grade for my essay.

 ISBN 978-81-8477-753-6

3. Jane leant forward to smell the roses.
4. They were looking for a shady place to sit.
5. Sam had never tasted goat's cheese before.

F
1. Paul is in the bathroom.
2. The children were entertained by a clown.
3. Mary was taller than Kate when they were younger.
4. The study is used as a bedroom when guests are staying overnight.
5. Sally is a better tennis player than her brother is.
6. The boat was full of people who were going on holiday.
7. I could not finish the jigsaw because some of the pieces were missing.
8. This is the dress I am wearing for Sue's wedding.
9. Some of the workers are unpaid and others are paid very little.
10. The programme was interesting but it went on for too long.

G It was Tom's birthday, and some of his friends were coming for lunch. He decided to make some soup with the vegetables that grew in his garden. He was not a very good cook, but he had found a recipe on the Internet that sounded easy enough.

The recipe told him to chop the vegetables and cook them in water until they went soft. Then he had to blend the mixture in the food processor. He did this, but unfortunately, he forgot to put the lid on the food processor before turning it on. The contents went all over the kitchen, and Tom began to feel rather stressed.

He cleared up the mess then began again. This time he had more success. The soup did not look very appetizing, but it smelt delicious. Tom tasted the soup and decided that it needed a bit more salt. He tried to sprinkle just a little into the pan, but the top came off the container and far too much fell in. The soup became very salty indeed. In fact, it was inedible.

Tom grew even more frustrated and annoyed. He did not have enough time or ingredients to make any more soup. So he took a couple of pizzas out of the freezer and cooked those instead.

Unit 5: Infinitives

A
1. fit 2. rain 3. run
4. touch 5. enjoy 6. stay
7. break 8. steal 9. be
10. pass

B *Possible answers:*
1. give 2. meet 3. call
4. sell 5. depart 6. drop
7. shake 8. speak 9. read
10. bite

C eat, try, bring, find, go, swim, like, miss, be, ride, teach, sew, put, win, close, mend, wear

D *Possible answers:*

Jane did not **eat** all her lunch.
The instructor made me **try** again.
I shall **bring** my holiday photos to show you.
Dad cannot **find** his car keys.
The wasp would not **go** away.
We watched the man **swim** across the river.
Does Joe **like** pizza?
Your family will **miss** you while you're away.
This might **be** our only opportunity.
Carol let me **ride** her new bike.
Parents should **teach** their children to be polite.
Tom can knit but he cannot **sew**.
Where shall I **put** these dishes?
Did you **win** the competition?
I heard someone **close** the door.
Mum makes us **mend** our own clothes.
You must **wear** strong shoes for the hike.

E
1. buy 2. run 3. be
4. have 5. lie 6. fly
7. go 8. leave 9. see
10. say

F
1. to read 2. know 3. to rest
4. to drink 5. tell 6. feel
7. to phone 8. hurt 9. take
10. to stay

G *Possible answers:*
1. to sit 2. to finish 3. to start
4. to wear 5. to leave 6. to tease
7. to play 8. to rain 9. to give
10. to answer

H If you are keen to become a doctor, you must work hard at school. You need to pass all your exams so that you may go to medical school. It is particularly important to do well in science subjects such as biology and chemistry.

A good doctor will also have a caring personality. He or she should want to help people get well. Being a doctor is not easy, but it can be a very rewarding career for the right person.

I
1. I tried to lift the box but it was too heavy.
2. Paul did not come to my party.
3. They decided not to buy the car.
4. Jane's teacher made her rewrite her essay more neatly.
5. You ought not to be rude to your parents.
6. I told her that she need not bring a sleeping bag.
7. Did Aunt Mary forget your birthday again?
8. Dad prefers not to drive in wet weather.
9. The dog does not want to go out.
10. The doctor advised the patient to eat more healthy food.

Unit 6: The Past Perfect Tense

A
1. written 2. begun
3. flown 4. sung
5. overtaken 6. thrown
7. run 8. seen
9. eaten 10. spoken
11. undone 12. trodden

B had … travelled, had remembered, had … forgotten, had come, had visited, had done, had brought, had … finished, had put, had arrived

C
1. found, had stopped
2. had taught, retired
3. sold, had stolen
4. noticed, had cleared
5. had risen, got
6. had brought, was
7. gave, had bought
8. had promised, forgot
9. had dropped, took
10. told, had won
11. sat, had cleaned
12. had locked, tried

D
1. never 2. just 3. already
4. just 5. never 6. already
7. already 8. just 9. never
10. already 11. just 12. never

E
1. Paul said (that) it had rained all week.
2. Sue told her brother (that) she had bought him a present.
3. Michael said (that) the baby had just woken up.
4. Alice complained that nobody had offered to help.
5. Joe said (that) he had spent all the money he had earned.
6. Mum asked me if I had finished my homework.
7. The boy protested that he had not understood the question.
8. My sister said (that) she had just had a phone call from someone she didn't know.

 ISBN 978-81-8477-753-6

9. Sue explained that she had been too ill to go to the party.
10. Sally asked David where he had put the milk he had bought.

F *Possible answers:*
2. the insect had bitten him.
3. my watch had stopped.
4. she had taken the medicine.
5. everyone had finished eating.
6. she had painted.
7. everyone had stopped talking.
8. he had not eaten since breakfast.
9. they had caught the thief.
10. my sister and I had gone to bed.
11. the battery had gone flat.
12. they had picked.
13. I had eaten my breakfast.
14. she had broken her doll.

Unit 7: Types of Adjectives and Their Order

A **Size**: deep, low, tiny, tall, thick
Quality: clever, different, old, popular, rude
Shape: oblong, round, square, straight, triangular
Colour: blue, brown, grey, red, white
Origin: American, Chinese, European, Italian, Pakistani
Material: metal, leather, paper, plastic, woollen

B
1. round 2. European
3. deep 4. Popular
5. red 6. old
7. metal 6. blue
9. tall 10. Chinese
11. plastic 12. straight

C *Possible answers:*
large, grey, rough, long, strong, heavy, wooden, curved, pointed, white, triangular, African

D *Possible answers:*
2. This plant has **red** berries. **(colour)**
3. The **tiny** insect crawled up the wall. **(size)**
4. Jane brushed her **curly** hair. **(shape)**
5. The **naughty** children were punished. **(quality)**
6. He works in a **Japanese** car factory. **(origin)**
7. I put the apples in a **paper** bag. **(material)**
8. She left a **short** note for her mother. **(size)**
9. Tom was wearing his **new** jacket. **(quality)**
10. There was a **round** mirror in every room. **(shape)**
11. I found a **silver** coin on the ground. **(material)**.
12. Jack does not like **English** cheese. **(origin)**

E
1. thin cotton
2. thick yellow
3. exciting, dangerous
4. busy English
5. purple and orange
6. huge modern concrete
7. small rectangular white
8. long, straight and black
9. polite, honest, intelligent (*Or* polite, intelligent, honest)
10. cold, tired and wet (*order of adjectives does not matter but comma and* ***and*** *must be added*)

F *Possible answers:*
1. Shakespeare is a famous English writer.
2. There is a small oval window in the door.
3. Alice put on her new black dress.
4. They built a high brick wall around the garden.
5. My cat has soft white fur.
6. A narrow winding path leads down to the lake.
7. The pyramids are huge Egyptian tombs.
8. The cannon fired heavy metal balls.
9. I had itchy red spots on my arms and legs.
10. He lay down in the long green grass.

G
1. Mum was knitting a warm woollen scarf.
2. My young English cousin is coming to stay.
3. The soup was hot, spicy and delicious.
4. She was wearing large round gold earrings.
5. Dad showed us a black and white photo of Grandma as a child.

Unit 8: Forming Adjectives from Verbs

A
1. ing 2. ive 3. ent
4. ed 5. ant 6. ive
7. ant 8. able 9. ed
10. ing 11. ent 12. ible

B
1. adhesive 2. admirable
3. affirmative 4. agreeable
5. appalling 6. comprehensible
7. controllable 8. convalescent
9. crying 10. debatable
11. digestible 12. excellent
13. explosive 14. forcible
15. imaginative 16. knotted
17. manageable 18. observant
19. staggering 20. tolerant
21. decorative 22. defiant
23. variable 24. worried

C
1. Indulgent 2. reliable
3. Surprising 4. reversible
5. Winning 6. recurrent
7. Decisive 8. married
9. Creative 10. knitted
11. hesitant 12. regrettable

D bored, delighted, pleasant, sensible, impressive, valuable, informative, framed, adorable, attractive, urgent, fascinating

E
1. freezing 2. amazing
3. fallen 4. exciting
5. depressed 6. annoying
7. frozen 8. interesting
9. disgusted 10. falling
11. excited 12. depressing
13. amazed 14. interested
15. disgusting 16. annoyed

F *Possible answers:*
1. It is advisable to wear a helmet when cycling.
2. 'Smaller' is a comparative adjective.
3. This is a very complicated puzzle.
4. Young children are dependent on their parents.
5. Odd numbers are not divisible by two.
6. An expectant mother is going to have a baby.
7. They went home the following morning.
8. I looked up at the glittering stars.
9. He made some rather offensive remarks.
10. My little sister can be very persuasive and she usually gets her own way.
11. I have just had some upsetting news.
12. Cotton and linen are woven fabrics.

Unit 9: Comparison of Adverbs

A
1. Dad has been driving more carefully since his accident.
2. Speak louder so that those sitting furthest from the stage can hear you.
3. The wind blew more strongly during the night.
4. They had a competition to find out who could stay silent the longest.
5. You will feel warmer if you walk more quickly.
6. Paul was the most smartly dressed boy in the room.
7. Jane moved closer to the front of the classroom in order to see the board better.
8. Some stars shine more brightly than others.
9. Those who wrote the most neatly got the highest marks in the handwriting test.

 ISBN 978-81-8477-753-6

10. The engine runs more smoothly when the car is newly serviced.

B 2. badly, worse, worst
3. long, longer, longest
4. gently, more gently, most gently
5. far, further, furthest
6. helpfully, more helpfully, most helpfully
7. fast, faster, fastest
8. noisily, more noisily, most noisily
9. hard, harder, hardest
10. enthusiastically, more enthusiastically, most enthusiastically
11. comfortably, more comfortably, most comfortably
12. well, better, best

C 1. low
2. more densely
3. loudest
4. better
5. bravely
6. worse
7. often
8. most generously
9. more kindly
10. thinly
11. furthest
12. fastest

D 1. most slowly 2. late
3. slowly 4. latest
5. more quickly 6. earlier
7. quickly 8. later
9. early 10. more slowly
11. earliest 12. most quickly

E earlier, hard, closest, further, more heavily, soundly, worst, better, higher, sooner

F *Possible answers:*
1. They began work more eagerly the following morning.
2. Answer the questions as honestly as you can.
3. Vegetables are sold the most cheaply at the market.
4. You must try harder next time.
5. I could do this sum more easily with a calculator.
6. This pen does not write as well as that one does.
7. Paul was standing the closest to the door.
8. You should speak more politely to your teacher.
9. The dog growled again, more angrily this time.
10. The children sang as sweetly as nightingales.
11. Those who have waited the longest should be served first.
12. The room is not as nicely decorated as it was for Paul's party.

Unit 10: Adverbial Phrases

A 1. I went to bed and fell asleep straight away.
2. The man hit the nail with a hammer and drove it into the wood.
3. This time last week we were sitting on the beach.
4. You have only just missed the bus. It left two minutes ago.
5. Last August I flew to England to visit my relatives.
6. They worked hard all morning and finally finished at midday.
7. In cold countries people dress more warmly when they go out.
8. My best friend has moved to another town so I see her less often than I used to.
9. Yesterday afternoon our teacher took us to the museum.
10. We arrived too early so we had to wait outside the cinema.

B 1. hardly ever
2. three times a day
3. after lunch
4. On Saturday mornings
5. at a restaurant
6. by the phone
7. for several weeks
8. into small pieces
9. Little by little
10. Fifty years ago
11. very reluctantly
12. during the performance

C Tom has been learning the violin **since his tenth birthday (D)**, when he received the instrument as a birthday present. **Once a week (F)** he has a violin lesson **at home (P)**. His teacher, Miss Lee, comes **to his house (P) on Friday evenings (T)**. She has been playing the violin **for many years (D)** and has performed **at the city's concert hall (P) several times (F)**. Needless to say, she plays **much more skilfully (M)** than Tom does **at the moment (T)**. However, he practises **very hard (M) every day (F)** before he goes **to school (P)**. He gets up **at 6.30 (T)** and plays his violin **from 7 to 8 a.m. (D) in his bedroom (P)**. His sister **quite often (F)** knocks **on the wall between their rooms (P)** and asks him to play **more quietly (M)** so that she can sleep **a little longer (D)**.

D 1. over there
2. extremely fast
3. straight home
4. last year
5. to work
6. at midnight
7. quite politely
8. tomorrow evening
9. for hours
10. more casually
11. since September
12. in bed

E *Possible answers:*
1. I am learning English at school.
2. I can walk ten kilometres without difficulty.
3. I sometimes watch TV during the evening.
4. I go to the dentist's twice a year.
5. I very rarely make any spelling mistakes.
6. I get up at half past seven.
7. I saw a good film at the cinema last week.
8. I usually do my homework in my bedroom.
9. I cannot paint very well.
10. I sleep for eight hours most nights.

F *Possible answers:*
1. I washed the porcelain vase **very carefully**.
2. The boys were playing football **in the park**.
3. They carried the injured player **off the field** on a stretcher.
4. She **rather nervously** asked him to repeat the question.
5. I am having a party **on my birthday**.
6. Jane ran **down the path** to greet her grandparents.
7. Dad has a shower **every morning** before breakfast.
8. **Last Sunday** it rained all day.
9. We learnt about polar bears **at school** today.
10. The phone rang several times **during the evening**.

Unit 11: Complex Prepositions

A 1. We lost the match because of Jane's poor performance in goal.
2. You had better keep away from me in case you catch my cold.
3. There has been an improvement in exam results compared with those of previous years.
4. My little brother has just learnt to count up to a hundred.
5. People pay different amounts of tax depending on their income.
6. The caretaker has all the keys other than the one for this room.
7. According to the timetable the train should arrive at 7:50.
8. Alternative sources of energy such as solar power do less harm to the environment.
9. There was no furniture in the room apart from the chair I was sitting on.

 ISBN 978-81-8477-753-6

10. The boy jumped on to the train as it moved away.
11. He made several mistakes owing to his lack of experience.
12. The food we have bought, together with what we already have, will be more than enough.

B
1. front 2. far
3. means 4. relation
5. reference 6. accordance
7. comparison 8. top
9. addition 10. case
11. well 12. aid

C on board – aboard; close to – near; in favour of – for; other than – except; in spite of – despite; by means of – by; next to – beside; on top of – on; prior to – before; but for – without; with regard to – about; out of – from

D *Possible answers:*
The pirates climbed on board the ship.
The people sitting close to the front had the best view.
Not many people voted in favour of changing the law.
Nobody other than Paul knew the answer to the question.
We went for a walk in spite of the rain.
The machine is prevented from overheating by means of a built-in fan.
Mark sits next to his best friend in class.
I put a cherry on top of each cake.
Prior to the operation she could not walk.
We would have arrived an hour ago but for the heavy traffic.
Mary said nothing with regard to what had happened.
The magician pulled a rabbit out of the hat.

E
1. to 2. of 3. with
4. from 5. to 6. on
7. for 8. between 9. with
10. as 11. of 12. from

F on behalf of; with regard to; next to; as well as; in spite of; in favour of; instead of; such as; close to; In view of

G *Possible answers:*
1. in spite of 2. due to
3. except for 4. out of
5. in between 6. on to
7. in case of 8. instead of
9. as well as 10. up to
11. close to 12. next door to

Unit 12: Prepositional Phrases

A The president arrived at the electronics factory in a large black car. The owners of the company, Mr and Mrs Kim, were waiting by the door to greet him. Their important visitor arrived on time, at exactly ten o'clock.

Mr and Mrs Kim invited the president into their office for coffee before his tour of the factory. Then they showed him around the main building, where their most complex products are made. He chatted to the workers and seemed very interested in the manufacturing process.

As he left, the president said that he was extremely impressed by Mr and Mrs Kim's company. He said it was the most efficiently run factory he had visited during his three years as president.

B
1. The spider crawled – up the wall.
2. My brother is – at work.
3. Jane apologized – for her mistake.
4. Please give this letter – to your parents.
5. The boat sailed – under the bridge.
6. Peter would like an apple – instead of a banana.
7. Mr Smith played the tune – on the piano.
8. Several people were absent – due to sickness.
9. We went for a walk – by the river.
10. I have not seen Michael – since last April.
11. The boy was eating a large slice – of cake.
12. Alice is taller – than Kate.

C
1. **out of** her purse
2. **for** them
3. **from** Sally
4. **about** football
5. **On** Saturday
6. **off** the road … **with** a tree
7. **next to** mine
8. **without** flour
9. **to** herself
10. **away from** the city centre **because of** the noise and traffic
11. **in** a grey suit … **at** the bank
12. **above** the fireplace … **by** my uncle

D
1. Adv 2. Adj 3. Adj
4. Adv 5. Adv 6. Adv
7. Adj 8. Adj 9. Adv
10. Adj 11. Adv 12. Adj

E *Possible answers:*
1. until ten o'clock
2. off his bike
3. down the hillside
4. with a smile
5. to my friend
6. around her neck
7. in the next room
8. under my bed
9. over the sleeping child
10. outside our house
11. about space travel
12. at university

F *Possible answers:*
1. She cut the rope with a sharp knife.
2. Mr Brown took his young son to the zoo.
3. Your clean jeans are in your wardrobe.
4. We have to write an essay about our holidays.
5. The lid of the box is over there.
6. I have never been to America.
7. He has not eaten anything since this morning.
8. The children hid behind the sofa and waited.
9. David felt ill during the English lesson.
10. Travelling by train is better for the environment.
11. A woman wearing a big hat was sitting in front of me.
12. We had chicken curry for lunch today.

G *(answers to questions 2, 5 and 7 would not be incorrect with the phrases in reverse order)*
1. in the apartment | above ours
2. up the lane | on his new bike
3. at the end | of the letter
4. to the birds | on the lake
5. in the garden | until sunset
6. to the man | at the gate
7. from her trip | with a bad cold
8. about road safety | by the policeman

Unit 13: Phrasal Verbs

A
1. run through 2. agree with
3. grow out of 4. call on
5. bring back 6. pull together
7. care for 8. give away
9. do away with 10. fall for
11. die down 12. carry out

B
1. put out – extinguish
2. take after – be like
3. draw up – write
4. stand for – represent
5. keep up with – go as fast as
6. change into – become
7. break down – stop working
8. go in for – enter
9. block off – close completely
10. carry on – continue
11. leave behind – forget to take
12. tell apart – distinguish between

C *Possible answers:*
1. The firemen managed to put out the fire.
2. Tom takes after his father, who is a professional musician.

 ISBN 978-81-8477-753-6

3. Carol drew up a guest list for her party.
4. The letter 'I' in the abbreviation stands for 'International'.
5. He was walking so fast that I could not keep up with him.
6. Caterpillars change into butterflies.
7. The washing machine has broken down again.
8. Are you going in for the photography competition?
9. The police blocked off the road after the accident.
10. He carried on working although he was very tired.
11. Someone has left their umbrella behind.
12. Nobody can tell the twins apart.

D 1. P 2. A 3. A
4. P 5. A 6. A
7. P 8. A 9. P
10. P 11. A 12. P

E 1. out 2. between
3. of 4. down
5. off 6. up
7. into 8. round
9. apart 10. from

F look, woke, got, set, lay, attend, fallen, picked, go, stood, passed, came

G 1. in, off 2. up, out
3. off, back 4. forward, up
5. back, in 6. up, at
7. out, around 8. over, away
9. in, down 10. out, up

H *Possible answers:*
1. made 2. speak 3. pulled
4. blow 5. add 6. dresses
7. brought 8. catch 9. Put
10. took

Unit 14: Conjunctions

A 1. before 2. and 3. until
4. or 5. unless 6. so
7. since 8. but 9. because
10. while

B 1. or 2. but 3. so
4. but 5. and 6. so
7. or 8. and 9. but
10. or 11. and 12. so

C 1. if 2. unless
3. even though 4. until
5. than 6. before
7. as 8. in case
9. even if 10. so that
11. since 12. because

D *Possible answers:*
but, or, and, if, when, because, until, while, although, unless

E 1. CC 2. P 3. SC
4. P 5. CC 6. CC
7. SC 8. P 9. CC
10. SC 11. SC 12. P

F *Possible answers:*
1. I could not get in
2. she had not been listening
3. it is clear
4. we had more money
5. can you do it yourself
6. the sun was not shining
7. you press this button
8. I have not seen it yet
9. nobody had heard him
10. she could
11. went to bed
12. you have your parents' permission

Unit 15: Transitional Devices

A
1. My parents lived in a tiny apartment before I was born.
2. Ali does not speak English. He can, however, speak several other languages.
3. If the phone rings while I am out, please take a message.
4. Carol invited Paul to her party but he could not go.
5. You must leave the building as soon as you hear the fire alarm.
6. All the doors were locked. Therefore, the burglar must have got in through a window.
7. Dad put on his glasses in order to read the small print on the document.
8. It rained every day and the food in the hotel was not very good. It was a disappointing holiday, all in all.
9. Most of these children are orphans. That is, they have no mothers or fathers.
10. You may have a cookie provided that you do not drop any crumbs on the carpet.
11. There were no melons on the fruit stall so Mum bought a pineapple instead.
12. First I mixed some fertilizer into the soil, then I sowed the seeds.

B 1. either … or 2. such … that
3. neither … nor 4. so … that
5. neither … nor 6. either … or
7. such … that 8. so … that
9. either … or 10. so … that
11. such … that 12. neither … nor

C *Possible answers:*
1. I don't have time to watch the film. Besides, I have seen it before.
2. You could sew a patch over the hole in your jeans. Alternatively, you could cut off the legs and turn them into shorts.
3. Mary wrote her name as neatly as she could.
4. The book is rather long, but it's a really exciting story.
5. A spider has eight legs whereas insects have only six legs.
6. Jane is a vegetarian. In other words, she does not eat meat.
7. The children were so excited that they could not sleep.
8. I washed the towels, then I hung them outside to dry.
9. The man was at home with his family. Therefore he could not have committed the robbery.
10. Michael took off his jumper because he was too hot.
11. We stood on the wall so that we could see over the heads of the crowd.
12. Sally will be very disappointed if she does not win a prize.

D while, Before, and, When, so, that, instead, such as, or, however, As soon as, First, then, Meanwhile, in order that, Otherwise, after, as

E *Possible answers:*
1. We have no eggs **so** I cannot make an omelette.
2. Uncle James is an architect. **That is**, he designs buildings.
3. Take a first-aid kit with you **in case** someone has an accident.
4. He kept chopping at the trunk with his axe. The tree fell down **eventually**.
5. **As soon as** the doorbell rang, Sally ran to the door.
6. **Although** the sun was shining, they stayed indoors all day.
7. Jack forgot his passport. **Consequently**, he could not get on the plane.
8. I searched my bedroom **but** I could not find my watch anywhere.
9. Alice felt sick **because** she had eaten too much.
10. Tom played the guitar **and** Billy played the drums.

Unit 16: Punctuation: Commas and Semicolons

A Mary was doing her homework when she heard a crash and a scream. Looking out of the window, she saw a man lying on the ground beside a fallen ladder. It was Joe Smith, her next-door neighbour. She ran outside to help him.

'What happened, Joe?' she asked. He replied, 'I was cleaning my upstairs windows and the ladder slipped. I think I may have broken my leg. Can you call an ambulance for me, please?' Mary returned to her

 ISBN 978-81-8477-753-6

house and spoke to her mother, who was in the kitchen. 'Joe Smith has had an accident,' she said.

While her mother phoned for an ambulance, Mary went back outside to make Joe more comfortable. She took him a blanket, a cushion for his head and a cool, refreshing glass of water. About ten minutes later, the ambulance arrived. They took Joe to the hospital to have his leg X-rayed.

Meanwhile, Mary's mother phoned Joe's wife, a nurse at the hospital, to tell her what had happened. She said that she would go straight to the emergency department to see her husband.

B
1. David asked, 'Do you think it will rain today?'
2. The bookstore also sells newspapers, magazines, paper, pens and cards.
3. The bride was wearing a long white dress.
4. 'You have made several spelling mistakes,' said the teacher.
5. Please do not walk on the grass.
6. I bought a ripe, juicy melon and some large red apples.
7. The man who wrote this book was at school with my father.
8. Neither Paul nor his brother knew where their mother was.
9. Alice is a polite, well-behaved girl.
10. Wearing only his pyjamas, he ran out of the house.
11. The prize, a silver trophy, will be given to the team which answers the most questions correctly.
12. However, there was no phone number on the advertisement in the newspaper.

C *Possible answers:*
1. I have invited Jane, Sue and Kate to my party.
2. The guide said, 'This castle is five hundred years old.'
3. 'I have finished my homework,' said John.
4. The children had happy, smiling faces.
5. Stop talking, please.
6. That is a lovely picture, Sally.
7. Yes, I can see the helicopter.
8. Tom, come and look at this strange insect.
9. As a result, the building collapsed.
10. If you notice anything suspicious, tell the police.
11. This photo was taken in York, a city in northern England.
12. My cousin Anna, who is a flight attendant, has travelled all over the world.

D
1. Leopards and tigers**, members of the cat family,** use the markings on their bodies for camouflage.
2. The music is by Beethoven**, a famous German composer**.
3. People **who wear glasses** are either long-sighted or short-sighted.
4. The Arctic Ocean**, where polar bears live**, is covered with ice.
5. You should not eat too much sugar**, which is bad for your teeth**.
6. There is enough food for everyone **who needs it**.
7. Mr Smith**, our English teacher,** comes from New York.
8. I showed my picture to Mum**, who said it was very good**.
9. Penguins**, which cannot fly,** use their flippers for swimming.
10. One of the rings **that were stolen** is very valuable.
11. Jane's new dress is red**, her favourite colour**.
12. I bought a DVD with the money **which you gave me**.

E
1. You will need the following items: a large square piece of wood; a box of nails; some black paint; and an assortment of tools, including a saw and a hammer.
2. Mum bought carrots, onions and tomatoes at the market; bread and cakes at the baker's; some meat at the butcher's; and a bouquet of lovely, sweet-smelling flowers for Grandma at the florist's.
3. I have invited ten people to my party: Carol, my best friend; four other friends from school; two of my cousins, Paul and Joe; and Tom, Kate and Sally, who live next door.
4. If a fire starts in the building, this is what you must do: sound the fire alarm; leave by the nearest exit; call the fire brigade; wait at some distance from the building, such as the far side of the car park.
5. We visited Buckingham Palace and the Tower of London on Monday; the National Art Gallery, the British Museum and Hyde Park on Tuesday; and Covent Garden, a busy shopping area, on Wednesday.
6. A healthy diet contains fresh fruit and vegetables, which are a good source of fibre; protein, which is found in meat, fish, eggs and milk; and carbohydrates for energy.

Unit 17: Punctuation: Hyphens, Dashes, Brackets and Ellipses

A Uncle Jack is my mother's brother-in-law. He is married to her sister, Aunt Julie. Uncle Jack has been a taxi-driver for twenty-five years. He loves his work and says that he would never want to do any other job. Sometimes it can be rather boring and frustrating, for example when he gets stuck in slow-moving traffic during the rush hour. However, at other times it can be quite exciting. One day he stopped beside a bank so that his passenger could use the cash-dispenser there. While he was waiting, a masked man carrying a gun ran out of the bank, knocking down a middle-aged woman on the pavement, and raced off down the street. Uncle Jack called the police on his mobile phone, then he and his passenger helped the passer-by who had been knocked down. Fortunately she was not badly hurt.

Aunt Julie is not so keen on her husband's job. Sometimes he works a sixteen-hour day, which means that he does not see much of their children. They have a four-year-old son, Ali, and twin daughters who are just six months old. Ali likes riding around with his father. He wants to become a taxi-driver as soon as he is old enough to take his driving test. Only fourteen years to wait!

B
1. English-speaking
2. cold-blooded
3. self-confidence
4. thirty-six
5. ten-minute
6. break-in
7. ear-piercing
8. hair-dryer
9. part-time
10. runner-up
11. long-awaited
12. take-off

C sis | ter, move | ment, win | ner, bath | room, in | cor | rect, soft | ly, hap | pi | ness, use | less, un | der | neath, plas | tered, con | ven | tion, sig | nal | ling

D *(the answers may be in a different order)*

2. Peter might know the answer – do you have his phone number?
3. Help yourselves to food and drink – there's plenty for everybody.
4. The car won't start – the battery must be flat.
5. Mum is cross with my brother – he spilt cola on the new rug.

 ISBN 978-81-8477-753-6

6. Jane looks nice – I wonder where she bought that dress.
7. Sam was not at school today – he has a bad cold.
8. It's time for lunch – there's a nice restaurant near here.

E 1. Carol Smith **(**a girl in our class**)** can swim ten lengths of the pool.
2. The book cost 540 rupees **(**about six dollars**)**.
3. They have four children **(**two girls and two boys**)** and numerous pets.
4. Mum's birthday **(**24 March**)** falls on a Saturday this year.
5. I walked from Orchard Lane **(**the street where I live**)** to Castle Towers **(**the apartment block where my grandparents live**)**.
6. Use a ruler **(**if you have one**)** to draw a line down the middle of the page.
7. Nobody likes Mark Jones, **(**a**)** because he is a bully and **(**b**)** because he tells lies.
8. We saw a huge bird **(**possibly an eagle**)** swoop down from the sky.
9. Light enters your eyes through the pupils **(**the dark holes in the middle**)**.
10. Miss Lee gave me an A **(**the highest mark**)** for my essay on Captain Cook **(**an 18th-century explorer**)**.

F 1. I opened Paul's present **(a Harry Potter DVD)** last of all.
2. The water is heated by solar power **(energy from the sun)**.
3. The birds use their talons **(large claws on their feet)** to seize their prey.
4. The fabric is turquoise **(greenish-blue)** with white strips.
5. Alice met Brad Pitt **(a famous actor)** while she was in New York.
6. Most of the furniture was made of mahogany **(a dark-coloured wood)**.
7. My English cousin is six feet **(about 1.8 metres)** tall.
8. The ring had a large red stone **(probably a ruby)** surrounded by diamonds.
9. Carnivorous **(meat-eating)** animals have sharp pointed teeth.
10. We watched a documentary about the Sahara **(an African desert)**.

G 2. As someone once said, 'Money … cannot make you happy.'
3. The saying 'Don't count your chickens …' comes to mind.
4. The president said, 'This new resort … will restore prosperity to the region.'
5. Remember the saying 'Sticks and stones may break your bones …' and ignore their cruel remarks.
6. The policeman said, 'The accident … could have been prevented.'

Unit 18: Phrases, Clauses and Sentences

A 1. Joe walked to school with his best friend.
2. There is nothing interesting on television today.
3. A man with a bad cough was sitting behind me on the bus.
4. A cheetah can run faster than any other animal.
5. You will find the dictionary on the top shelf of the bookcase.
6. A very tall woman was standing behind the counter.
7. Sally gave her sister a box of chocolates for her birthday.
8. The person responsible must be punished for this terrible crime.
9. Mum put a mat under the hot dish.
10. Tom lay on his back on the grass looking up at the fluffy white clouds in the sky.
11. Last year we went to England for three weeks.
12. Mary told me a secret and I promised not to tell anyone else.

B in a business suit, their friends and relatives, one by one, all alone, his mobile phone, to the station, very long, at her watch, extremely slowly, an empty parking space, A few minutes later, hand in hand

C *Possible answers:*

Noun phrases: A young man; a business suit; a large suitcase; the train; the platform; a familiar face; the people; their friends and relatives; *etc.*

Adjectival phrases: in a business suit; all alone; rather self-conscious; very long; beside a row of shops; really pleased; so worried

Adverbial phrases: off the train; along the platform; the previous evening; on a seat; one by one; at her watch; extremely slowly; hand in hand; *etc.*

Prepositional phrases: among the people; for him; on the busy street; to the station; in a very long traffic jam; on the station platform; for a week; to the parked car; *etc.*

D

1. P	2. C	3. C
4. P	5. P	6. C
7. P	8. C	9. C
10. P		

E *Possible answers:*
1. Mum bought me a book about dinosaurs.
2. People who work hard deserve to do well.
3. Name some of the animals you saw at the zoo.
4. The sun was shining when we left.
5. This is the tallest building in the country.
6. Can you run as fast as Mary can?
7. Dad rather foolishly left his wallet lying on the table.
8. Bicycles have two wheels but most cars have four wheels.
9. Did you paint any of these pictures?
10. Go away and leave me alone!

Unit 19: Main Clauses and Subordinate Clauses

A

1. S	2. M	3. M
4. S	5. M	6. M
7. S	8. M	9. M
10. S	11. S	12. M
13. S	14. S	15. M
16. S		

B 1. Dad cleaned the house – while Mum was at the shops.
2. I showed my friend the photos – that I had taken.
3. When the apples are ripe – we shall pick them.
4. This is the boy – whose bicycle has been stolen.
5. If you eat too much – you will get fat.
6. Mary had a cousin – who could do magic tricks.
7. Take some money with you – in case you need to get a taxi home.
8. Although Ali lives in England – he cannot speak English.
9. Sue switched on the lamp – so that she could see better.
10. Because the children had done well – they were each given a reward.
11. Farmers sell most of the crops – that they grow.
12. I shall not phone you – unless I am going to be late.

C There was a serious accident on the expressway yesterday morning. The road was very busy because many people were on their way to work. There was also a lot of rainwater on the road, which made the surface slippery. A truck had a puncture and stopped suddenly. The car behind it, which was going too fast, crashed into it. When other drivers saw this, some of them slowed down. However, those who were not paying enough attention drove straight into the back of the

 ISBN 978-81-8477-753-6

vehicles in front of them. There was a huge pile-up.

The driver of the truck, who was unhurt, phoned the emergency services. As soon as they received the call they sent the police and an ambulance to the scene. They also sent a fire engine in case any of the vehicles caught fire. The police closed the expressway so that there would be no further collisions. Meanwhile, the ambulance crew attended to the people who were trapped in their cars. Miraculously, nobody was very badly hurt.

D
1. David does an hour's piano practice before he goes to school. *Or* Before he goes to school, David does an hour's piano practice.
2. Our principal, who does not have a car, comes to school by bus.
3. If you don't know the correct spelling(,) look up the word in a dictionary. *Or* Look up the word in a dictionary if you don't know the correct spelling.
4. My grandparents live in Karachi, which is a long way from here.
5. Mr Smith has two sons, whose names are Paul and Tom.
6. Nobody could read the writing because it was very untidy.
7. As I was getting dressed(,) I noticed a hole in one of my socks. *Or* I noticed a hole in one of my socks as I was getting dressed.
8. Sally gave the ball that she had found to her brother.
9. Most of the animals which live on the farm eat grass or hay.
10. Please buy me some shampoo while you are at the supermarket. *Or* While you are at the supermarket, please buy me some shampoo.

E *Possible answers:*
1. Nobody will hear you unless you speak more loudly.
2. The baby was asleep so I tiptoed out of the room.
3. A pilot is a person who flies a plane.
4. The sun went in and it began to rain.
5. Fruit and vegetables contain vitamins, which are good for you.
6. The thief ran away when the dog started barking.
7. Jack wanted an ice cream but he did not have enough money.
8. Everyone congratulated Jane, whose picture won first prize.
9. Tom kept on walking although his feet were sore.
10. You can share my bedroom or you can sleep on the sofa.
11. Alice cannot drink milk because she is allergic to it.
12. Mum cooked the fish that we had caught.
13. I waved to Mary but she did not see me.
14. You must cook this meat before you eat it.
15. The children were frightened so they ran away.
16. We gave our old toys to Mrs Green, who has four young children.

Unit 20: Simple, Compound and Complex Sentences

A S, Cd, S, Cx, Cx, Cd, Cx, S, Cx, Cx, Cd, Cd.

B *Possible answers:*
2. Anna closed the window before she drew the curtains.
3. The front tyre of my bicycle was flat so I pumped it up.
4. Bring a swimsuit in case we go swimming.
5. The car stopped and a smartly dressed man got out.
6. Uncle Jack never travels by air because he is afraid of flying.
7. Mrs Lee, who is a nurse, said I should have an anti-influenza injection.
8. Tom pushed the door but it did not open.
9. Mary entered the competition although she did not think she had much chance of winning it.
10. Should I glue the pieces together or should I use sticky tape?
11. As soon as his alarm clock went off, David leapt out of bed.
12. Mr and Mrs Jones, whose children have left home, are moving to a smaller house.

C *Possible answers:*
1. The thief ran out of the shop and disappeared into the crowd.
2. The pianist played a few wrong notes but nobody noticed.
3. They might be held up in traffic or they might have got lost.
4. The baby was crying so its mother picked it up.
5. At the weekend we visit our grandparents or go to the park.
6. Alice washed her hair and let it dry in the warm sunshine.
7. Paul was struggling with his homework so his sister helped him.
8. I would like to be a doctor but I don't think I am clever enough.
9. Carol sold her old camera and bought a new one.
10. John and Sue are going to a concert so they cannot come to the party.
11. Sally liked the black shoes best but they did not fit her.
12. You can phone the company or you can send them an email.

D *Possible answers:*
1. Mum was worried **because we were late**.
2. **Although I was bored,** I stayed till the end of the party.
3. You will not pass your exam **unless you work harder**.
4. **When the light goes out,** the battery is fully charged.
5. The photos **that I took on the boat** have not come out very well.
6. **If you are being bullied at school,** you should tell your teacher or your parents.
7. Joe has earned a lot of money **since he set up his window-cleaning business**.
8. This letter is from Peter, **who is on holiday in America**.
9. **While I was in the shopping mall** I noticed that a new bookstore had opened.
10. The old prison, **which closed in 1980,** has been converted into luxury apartments.
11. Grandpa felt much better **after he had his heart operation**.
12. **As nobody answered all the questions correctly,** we shall go over this topic again in the next lesson.

E *Possible answers:*
2. I live in a house.
3. A saw is a tool that is used for cutting wood.
4. You can fry it or you can roast it in the oven.
5. The show starts at seven o'clock.
6. I went into the bathroom and had a shower.
7. I am laughing because I have just read a funny story.
8. An orphan is a child whose parents have died.
9. He has a cold so he has to stay at home.
10. A spider has eight legs.
11. Please put them on that shelf.
12. No, I tried to phone her but she was out.

Unit 21: Active and Passive Voice

A
1. passive, past continuous
2. active, present perfect
3. active, present continuous

 ISBN 978-81-8477-753-6

4. passive, past perfect
5. active, past continuous
6. passive, past
7. active, past perfect
8. passive, present continuous
9. passive, present
10. active, future

B *Possible answers:*
1. The baby birds were being fed by their parents.
2. Have you shown Dad the model you made at school today?
3. The children are playing a video game.
4. The house had been built in the wrong place.
5. Carol was wearing her new necklace.
6. Medals were awarded to the winners.
7. I had never seen such a large fish before.
8. The fruit is being picked by a team of workers.
9. Dogs are not allowed in the museum.
10. Mum will be angry if we are late.

C
1. This tree was planted by my grandparents.
2. Wheat is not grown on this farm.
3. Were you told what to do?
4. It can be worn as a scarf or as a hood.
5. The cat was being chased by a large black dog.
6. I have not been invited to Sally and Tom's wedding.
7. Alice's get-well card had been signed by all her friends.
8. You will be given your test results tomorrow.

D *Possible answers:*
1. The security cameras are constantly filming the people inside the store.
2. The students at this school do not wear school uniform.
3. Colin's performance impressed the judges.
4. The police have arrested the thief.
5. The flood had swept several houses away.
6. Mrs Green will make the costumes for the play.
7. You can buy fresh fruit and vegetables at the market.
8. Nobody wants this scrap paper.

E *Possible answers:*
1. had forgotten
2. is being repaired
3. are used
4. will hurt
5. have been washed
6. were sailing
7. likes
8. were treated
9. are looking
10. had been sold

Unit 22: Direct and Indirect Speech

A *Possible answers:*
1. 'What are you laughing at?' I asked them.
2. 'I cannot make any bread,' said Mum, 'because I have no flour.'
3. 'I last saw my brother two weeks ago,' said Sally.
4. 'Did you see anything suspicious,' asked the policeman, 'or hear any strange noises?'
5. 'Do not stand too close to the edge,' said the guide.
6. 'My father is a doctor,' he said, 'and my mother is a teacher.'
7. 'Go and lie down in your cabin,' said the captain, 'if you feel seasick.'
8. 'I shall phone you as soon as I get off the train,' said Aunt Jane.

B *Possible answers:*
1. The man at the door ordered us to take off our muddy boots.
2. Dad promised that he would mend my bike the following day.
3. The customer enquired whether the picture in the window was for sale.
4. The doctor advised Grandma not to go out until she felt better.
5. The reporter asked when the accident had happened.
6. The station master informed me that the train to Springfield did not stop there.
7. Our hostess told us to help ourselves.
8. Miss Jones explained that the children could not understand what she was saying because they did not speak English.

C *Possible answer:*

'What are you doing, Dad?' asked Kate. Her father told her that he was making her mother a jewellery box for her birthday. 'It's a surprise,' he added, 'so don't tell her about it.'

Kate asked her father if she could do anything to help. 'Not really,' he replied, 'but you can watch me if you like.' 'Thank you,' said Kate. She asked her father the name of the tool he was using. He told her that it was called a fretsaw.

'Are you going to paint the box when you have finished it?' asked Kate. Her father said that he probably would. 'What colour will you paint it?' asked Kate. 'I have not decided yet,' replied her father.

Kate asked her father if she was annoying him with all her questions. 'Yes,' he said. He asked her to go away and leave him alone.

 ISBN 978-81-8477-753-6